Gay Marriage, Real Life

To Kristin
With much love
and best wishes,
Michelle
January 2006

Gay Marriage, Real Life

Ten Stories of Love and Family

Michelle Bates Deakin

SKINNER HOUSE BOOKS
BOSTON

Skinner House Books is an imprint of the Unitarian Universalist Association of Congregations, a liberal religious organization with more than 1,000 congregations in the U.S. and Canada. 25 Beacon Street, Boston, MA 02108-2800.

Printed in United States.

Cover art *April Light-Clothesline in Venice*, © 2003 Marian Dioguardi, http://refrigerator-art.org
Author photo by Larry Osgood.
Cover design by Kathryn Sky-Peck.
Text design by Suzanne Morgan.

ISBN 1-55896-491-6
978-1-55896-491-4

5 4 3 2 1
08 07 06 05

Library of Congress Cataloging-in-Publication Data

Deakin, Michelle Bates.
    Gay marriage, real life : ten stories of love and family / Michelle
Bates Deakin.
        p. cm.
    ISBN-13: 978-1-55896-491-4 (pbk. : alk. paper)
    ISBN-10: 1-55896-491-6 (pbk. : alk. paper)
    1. Same-sex marriage.   I. Title.
HQ1033.D43 2006
306.84'80973--dc22
                                        2005023219

Photo credits: Alicia Prickett (p. 14), Denise Schreiner (p. 50), Ainslie Pryor (p. 74), Lorene Hiris (p. 86), Mia Song (p.108).
Lyrics from "Everything Possible" by Fred Small, copyright 1983 Pine Barrens Music (BMI). Reprinted by permission.

To Deax,
Adam, and Charlie,
the loves of my life

Contents

Foreword

Fear follows the advance of gay rights like a shadow.

Every step of the way, as gays and lesbians push to widen the scope of their rights, they encounter resistance derived from fear. The idea of gay marriage goes to the root of that fear, which in many places has blossomed into fierce opposition.

At the same time, acceptance of gay relationships is growing broadly and rapidly across the nation. Ten years ago gay marriage was a distant hope. Now gay marriage is legal in Massachusetts, and civil unions are legal in Vermont and Connecticut. In addition, court cases are advancing in other states. Even so, the shadow of fear continues to accompany these steps, with numerous states passing or considering constitutional amendments to bar gay marriage. At the center of this nationwide struggle are people seeking the right to do something that is both ordinary and extraordinary. They want to marry.

The idea of gay marriage challenges traditional assumptions and threatens the authority of some religious teachings. This challenge and this threat inhere in the premise underlying the idea of gay marriage: that marriage is a committed, exclusive, loving relationship between two people and that the gender of one's partner is for each person to choose according to the dictates of the heart.

Stories from the heart are the best answer to the fears clouding the question of gay marriage. During the struggle for civil unions in Vermont, I watched as dozens of gay and lesbian Vermonters stepped forward to speak the truth about their lives. They put a human face on a contentious political issue. When 1,500 people gathered one winter evening at the Vermont State House to debate the question, many could see that the people speaking out about their lives and loves were ordinary Vermonters, living ordinary lives, seeking a right that most people take for granted and could readily understand—the right to marry the man or woman of their choosing. Their courage in speaking out in the face of wrathful opposition won them the admiration of many.

The stories in these pages put a human face on the issue in a similar way. The families in these stories experience confusion and heartache as they come to terms with the sexual orientation of a son, daughter, brother, sister. Sometimes families fail to come to terms, or, as in one devastating instance, death intervenes as a father reaches the very threshold of reconciliation.

These stories form a rich and varied tapestry. There are a Vietnam veteran and his partner, a Vietnamese refugee. There are a seminary student and her partner, a soldier in the National Guard. There are loving parents who take on the cause of their children and parents who come to acceptance painfully, or never. There are couples struggling in the South to be true to themselves in a culture that is not ready for them. There are children with two moms who wonder what the problem is.

For those who want a deeper understanding of why marriage is important to gay and lesbian couples, these moving accounts provide a good place to begin. Those with the courage to be open about the truth of their lives have enormous power to dispel fear and to show that love and marriage among gay and lesbian couples is not some other thing—it is love and marriage, and it is something we can all understand. The couples who agreed to tell their stories in this book provide a glimpse into the struggle gay and lesbian couples still face in securing a place in American life where their rights are honored and they are free to follow the ordinary and extraordinary pathways of love.

David Moats
Editorial Page Editor, *Rutland Herald*

Introduction

This is a book about love.

The stories in this book are small and enormous at the same time. Each gives us a glimpse of the everyday and miraculous journey of falling in love and weaving two lives together. These lovers are in same-sex couples. Like all loving unions, their relationships make the world a better, warmer place.

The courts in my home state of Massachusetts were the first—and as of this writing—the only to affirm same-gender marriage. Heterosexual marriages, like my own, have been wholly unaffected, despite the predictions from social conservatives that they would be tarnished or debased if same-sex couples received the civil and legal protections of equal marriage rights. Living where I do, in one of the most liberal towns in one of the country's most liberal states, it is sometimes easy to assume that the battle for equal marriage rights has been won. But we are less than one year past the startling election of 2004, in which voters across the United States turned out to vote in favor of same-sex marriage bans. And just a few miles from my church, where same-sex couples are now routinely joined in full legal marriage, a band of fundamentalists protests a picture book celebrating diverse families that is optional reading for kindergarten children in a local public school.

Even where gay marriage is fully legal, it is still a courageous act.

Some of the couples profiled are political activists who are lobbying for equal marriage and parenting rights for same-sex couples. Others are making the case for equal marriage rights just by openly living their lives together. Whether they are politically active or not, all of these couples help pave the way for gay marriage simply by being together. In that way, they show a neighbor, a coworker, or a cousin that same-sex love can be happy and beautiful. They teach teenagers not to be ashamed if they are attracted to same-gender friends. And they provide examples to small children who haven't yet learned to disbelieve that two moms or two dads can create a loving home.

All of the couples who shared their stories for this book are brave, even heroic. Their weapons in the crusade against hatred are their stories. It has been a poignant experience to hear similar stories coming from so many different people living such different lives. When many of these couples met, they didn't know whether they could spend their lives with each other. There were few role models to show them how. Now they have become role models themselves for the next generation. Their stories have the power to change the lives and loves of people of any sexual orientation. They are living the story of the transforming power of love.

Certainly it takes more than just stories to win a civil rights fight. The ongoing and indefatigable efforts of lawyers, activists, and legislators are essential. But gay couples living openly together are at least as important. They are creating public awareness and acceptance, one person at a time. Ultimately, these personal stories can create lasting change. Few people are moved by nameless and faceless injustice. But when people can put a face on gay marriage and see that that face has a loving smile, progress in the march toward social justice is made.

There are many differences among the people in this book. They hail from across the country, from Massachusetts, New Jersey, California, North Carolina, Georgia, Washington, Kansas, and Oklahoma. They are professors, businesspeople, students, artists, and engineers. They are from a variety of religious traditions—and from none at all. They are white, African-American, and Asian-American. One area in which I did not find diversity, however, was socioeconomic status and education. The people who feel safe telling their stories are solidly middle and upper-middle class. They know that if speaking out costs them a job, they have the skills and resources to find another. With this economic safety net, they know they are speaking out from a place of comfort, and several feel compelled by this understanding to tell their stories, for the sake of people who cannot.

Wherever possible, I have used the language preferences of those I interviewed. Some people like the term *gay marriage*; others don't. Some prefer *queer* to *gay*, while others regard *queer* as a slur. Couples varied in their choice of the words *partner*, *spouse*, *husband*, or *wife*. I have used a very liberal definition of *marriage* in selecting the couples for this book. There is only one couple, two men from Massachusetts, who are married in the eyes of their state. To expand the geographic scope, I have included couples from many different states. Some have had formal commitment ceremonies. Others have exchanged rings privately. One couple was briefly legally married in San Francisco before a California court ruled their union was invalid. And one couple is a plaintiff in a "Freedom to Marry" lawsuit in Washington. By the time this book is published, they may have prevailed in their lawsuit and be legally wed. I ask that readers overlook word choice even when the language does not jibe with their own particular sensibilities. My hope is that readers will embrace the spirit of this book, which is a celebration of love.

Clay and Rashad

*"There's something liberating
in speaking your truth."*

In the second row of the Tabernacle Baptist Church in northeast Atlanta, Clay Allen and Rashad Burgess are on their feet, hands raised toward the altar. "Preach!" Clay shouts among a chorus of voices ringing out in agreement with Rev. Dennis Meredith. "The Lord loves awlllll people," Pastor Meredith exclaims, stretching out the "all" to include everyone in the sun-drenched pews. "Even if you're practicing something"—he grins—"because we're all practicing something. If we're not practicing one thing, we're practicing something else."

Clay leans toward the preacher with outstretched arms. He steps out into the aisle, stomping his feet in an impassioned dance in front of the pulpit, praising the Lord with his body and soul for the affirmation that he is included and recognized as a beloved child of God. Rashad nods and smiles. Three rows of the gospel choir stand rapt behind Rev. Meredith. They clap and shout praise: "That's good!" "Preach, Preacher!"

Not even babies fall asleep in this service, where drums, an electric guitar, and three keyboards accompany a fifty-member choir making joyful noise unto the Lord. "Walk in the light," the choir leads, as a dozen congregants make their way to the front row to be saved. "Come where the dewdrops of mercy shine bright." Jumbo-sized boxes of Kleenex are passed freely around the hall as tears well up and roll down cheeks. "Shine all around us by day and by night, Jesus, the light of the world."

By the end of the two-and-one-half-hour service, ears are ringing from the volume and power of the music, and the air is thick with the spiritual passion that the preacher has unleashed. Worshippers are quaking and speaking in tongues, and the congregation is moved on this Palm Sunday to shout and sing and stomp and dance.

Clay and Rashad were both raised in the spirited traditions of African-American churches. Clay was brought up in his uncle's Pentecostal church in suburban Los Angeles, and Rashad belonged to a Baptist congregation in the southern suburbs of Chicago. Steeped in the spirit and power of black churches, neither could imagine giving up this kind of worship because they were gay or because they were married to each other.

Rashad and Clay

The Tabernacle Baptist Church, where the couple attended the Palm Sunday service, proclaims itself to be a "place of love and acceptance," welcoming to all, and Clay and Rashad do feel embraced by that community. But they are creating a new black church in Atlanta to reach out more directly to the gay community. Their new place of worship, The Vision Church, is slated to open on January 1, 2006. Clay and Rashad envision a Christ-centered ministry that fully embraces people of every sexual orientation, family configuration, race, gender, physical or mental condition, and "all other distinctions that are the rich tapestry of God's creation."

"It's a place for people who have been shut out by so many churches," says Clay, his gentle, almond-shaped brown eyes clear and hopeful, his warm smile punctuated on either side by sparkling diamond earrings. "There's a whole segment of people who grew up in the church and have been severely wounded. I have been called to speak to those people," he explains. A thirty-two-year-old student of philosophy and religion at Atlanta's Morehouse College, he has been preaching since he was twelve. Along with Rashad, a twenty-nine-year-old team leader with the Centers for Disease Control and Prevention (CDC), Clay wants to educate people through The Vision Church. "We're greater than our sexuality," he says. "We need to have a purpose to our lives that is larger than our gender. My ministry lies at the intersection of spirituality, social consciousness, sexuality, and specifically how our divine destiny is connected to them all."

Rashad and Clay were married on July 20, 2003, in Hilton Head, South Carolina, a golf and beach mecca that caters to white, upper-middle-class tourists. But Clay and Rashad were drawn to the luxury of an expensive resort for their carefully crafted ceremony. "We were the only colored people there, except for the folks who worked at the hotel," Rashad says, laughing. For the wedding, they were alone on the beach at sunrise.

They rose at 4:30 that Sunday morning and dressed in matching white dashikis and pants. (As hard as they had searched Atlanta, they couldn't find African clothes in white, but they finally found the flowing white outfits they had in mind in an Indian shop.) Rashad and Clay quietly crept from their hotel room in their white suits and headbands bearing a small carved wooden trunk and two wicker torches. On the beach, they unpacked their supplies and replaced the trunk's lid. The trunk was now an altar. They pushed the torches into the sand, lit them, and arranged their props, a mélange of elements from African culture and the Christian church. They placed a broom on the sand behind the altar and laid wine and bread on the altar for Communion, as well as candles, a bell, and a Bible, from which they read from Corinthians 13 about love. ("Love is patient, love is kind. Love is not jealous or boastful; it is not arrogant or rude. Love keeps no record of wrongs; it is not irritable or resentful; it does not rejoice at wrong, but rejoices in the right. Love bears all things, believes all things, hopes all things, endures all things.") From matching red velvet journals, they read their vows, words of love and commitment.

Rashad ReNard Richard Burgess vowed to Clay to be continually faithful, always honoring their covenant, never to leave him, never to leave angry, and to forsake all others. He ended with the West African equivalent of Amen, *Ashe*.

Oliver Clyde Allen III vowed to Rashad to be loyal and to protect him, to build him up, to comfort and soothe him, to provide and work hard for both of them, never to act in fear, to communicate his own heart's desire, to stand by Rashad's side, never to hurt Rashad out of anger or with malicious intent, and to give Rashad his body and soul. *Ashe*.

The two men exchanged matching white-gold rings, each set with a single row of diamonds, as the peach-colored sunrise turned to early morning light. Then they jumped the broom in the tradition of their enslaved ancestors. Dog walkers who had begun roaming the beach curiously eyed the two black men in flowing white garb beside their altar between two torches. A woman in her late sixties passed with a golden retriever on a leash. "Would you take our picture?" Clay and Rashad asked. The woman smiled and said, "Oh! Okay!"—and memorialized the event with a striking photo of two beaming, handsome men holding each other as husbands for the first time.

Clay and Rashad had toyed with the idea of a large wedding. "I bought all the wedding books and magazines," Clay says, laughing. But they realized they were facing a choice between a lavish wedding or a down payment on a house, and the house prevailed. They purchased a newly renovated Craftsman-style home in southwest Atlanta with sparkling hardwoord floors and stylish black stainless-steel appliances. As it turned out, they managed to have a reception as well. A few weeks before the wedding, Rashad had announced their plans to his coworkers at the CDC. His colleagues began to design a reception that grew to include church friends and Morehouse peers. More than 150 people gathered to fete Rashad and Clay on a hot July night before they drove to Hilton Head. They were toasted by friends and prayed over by Pastor Meredith. They fed each other slices of the elaborate two-tiered wedding cake a friend had prepared and read each other letters of commitment. "So many people thought it *was* the ceremony and told me it was the best wedding they'd ever been to," says Clay, recalling with a smile the overwhelming emotion of the send-off. "We didn't know that many people loved us."

Rashad and Clay are the kind of first-born, overachieving sons every mother dreams of raising. At twenty-nine, Rashad has risen to the management ranks of the CDC, leading national HIV-prevention programs. Clay is a member of two honor societies at Morehouse, the all-male African-American college that trained Martin Luther King Jr., civil rights leader Julian Bond, and film maker Spike Lee. Neither's choice of a partner, however, has garnered the same praise as his impressive intellectual and professional accomplishments.

In the Baldwin Hills area of Los Angeles, Clay grew up in an ultraconservative, ultrafundamentalist Christian home. "Everything was a sin," he recalls. By age twelve he was a youth minister in his uncle's Spirit of Life Christian church and under no illusion that the sexual attractions he was experiencing were sanctioned in that community. He spent years living a double life, engaged to a young lady but dating men. He grew increasingly depressed. "I was in the closet," Clay says, remembering the conflicts between his feelings and his religion. "I knew what I felt was a sin whether I acted on it or not. But it was safer to do it and believe it's a sin than to not do it."

Rashad nods, his shoulder-length dreadlocks bobbing in agreement, able to laugh now at the teachings that had also shaped his young life. "There's redemption as long as you know it's wrong. Otherwise you have a reprobate mind and a one-way ticket to hell."

At twenty-two, Clay told his mother he was struggling with being gay. He knew his mother was no stranger to gay culture. She was an active singer in the gospel music industry, and it's an open secret in the black community that gospel choirs and groups are full of gay men. But she reacted to her son's news with horror. Clay recalls how she gracefully left the room and retreated to her bedroom. There she buried her face in her pillow and started to scream.

That scene took place in 1997. Clay and his mother did not so much as broach the subject again until 2003, when Clay took a more direct approach. This time he didn't say he was struggling. Instead he told her, "Mom, I'm gay, and I'm going to marry Rashad."

The words moved like a nuclear explosion through the close-knit Allen family. Clay's uncle, who had welcomed him as an associate pastor in his church and was grooming him as his successor, told him he wasn't welcome in the pulpit anymore. His paternal aunt barred him from her house. His mother agonized over what to tell her friends and repeatedly asked him, "Why are you doing this to me?"

Clay was devastated. He was still reeling from the recent loss of two grandparents, an aunt, and his younger sister, LaTanya, who had been killed in a car crash at the age of twenty-one. The deaths had occurred within nine months of one another. The rejection of his remaining family was another searing loss.

But Clay knew he couldn't hide his life any longer. He had no intention of concealing traces of Rashad's presence when his mother came to visit. It was time to be truthful. Even amid the pain of rejection, his conversation with his mother brought him a kind of peace. "No matter how your family responds, there is something liberating when you say it," says Clay. "Something happens."

Rashad agrees. "There is something liberating in speaking your truth to your family. It's amazing when you come out to your mother. It's very freeing." So freeing for Rashad, in fact, that after he came out to his mother, he vowed he would never again be in the closet. "I didn't want to go through the pain of having to come out to anyone again."

The despair Rashad felt after coming out to his mother was fleeting. "I always knew I was gay," Rashad recalls, "but I always tried to hide it." As a teenager, he slowly began to receive more attention from admiring boys than from girls. His mother, to whom he's always been close, often questioned him. "Is that your boyfriend?" she'd ask. He would always say no, and the constant denials seemed to irritate his mother, who was just nineteen years older than her son and as much a buddy as a parent.

Rashad excelled in school and earned a place at the prestigious University of Chicago, where he experienced his first taste of an intellectual environment that didn't condemn homosexuality. Upon meeting one of Rashad's male college friends, Raymond, his mother once again frankly asked over the phone one day if Raymond was a boyfriend. This time, the question shocked Rashad. He dropped the phone, summoned his courage, and answered, "Yes." His mother simply said, "Okay."

Not long after that, on Easter Sunday, Rashad brought Raymond and two of his female friends to his family's church. His mother's delayed bitterness surfaced in the parking lot, where she started yelling at Rashad, "I can't believe you brought *him* here!" She made herself go inside the church, but she soon started to cry and ran out of the sanctuary and into the back room, where Rashad caught up with her. He told her, "This is who I am, and you have to accept that. This is who I've always been."

"I know," his mother said, "I just have to grieve a little. I love you."

She made her way back to the service. Rashad's family, and his friends—including Raymond—went out for Easter dinner, and his mother has accepted Rashad as a gay man ever since.

Rashad's impending marriage—not his homosexuality—drove a wedge between him and his father. (His parents had never married.)

Coincidently, Rashad broke the news to his father on another Easter Sunday. He was sitting at the table with his father's family when his cousin casually asked, "Are you dating anyone?"

"Yes," said Rashad. "As a matter of fact, we're getting married."

Forks dropped. The room froze. His grandmother's arm hung suspended in midair as she held a piece of half-eaten cornbread to her mouth.

His father, Ross Burgess, laughed. "Oh, Rashad. You're playing."

"No. I'm not. I am. And he's a preacher."

The chill that froze that Easter dinner with Rashad's family has never really thawed. Conversations with his father have dropped to one or two a year. When Rashad saw his grandmother the next Christmas Eve there was no hug for him. She shook his hand.

The two mothers, Mittie Dawson-Allen and Diane Bradley, met in Atlanta for the first time in the winter of 2004. Clay's mother, Mittie, had flown out from Los Angeles to attend a conference, and Diane was in town for a family weekend at Spelman College, where Rashad's sister was in school, and to see his brother, also a student at Morehouse.

There was another family dinner. Another awkward moment. The topic of homosexuality came up. "I don't condone it," said Mittie.

And the topic of gay marriage. "I don't embrace it," Mittie added.

Angry to the point of boiling, Rashad said nothing. Clay's mother had been a guest in their house for more than a week. They'd been having a wonderful time, laughing and seeing the sights. He was afraid to say anything at all for fear he wouldn't be able to stop at just a few words.

Instead, Rashad's mother calmly stepped in and explained her process of coming around to acceptance. "There was a time when I would have had a broom in my hand if I had seen Clay dropping off Rashad," Diane told Mittie. "But I cried a little, and I let some stuff go."

Clay is happy his mother could witness Diane's acceptance, and he hopes it will move his own mother along in her growth process. Just a year before, she had said she would never walk into their house, but here she was—a guest for ten days.

Rashad says, "I know Mittie loves Clay, and I know she loves me, and she can't deny that we authentically love each other. She got the chance to see another woman be loving and accepting of her son and embracing him. Whether or not she was changed by it, at least she saw it."

Creating The Vision Church seems to be where the lives of Clay and Rashad have always been leading, first individually and then together. Clay has been active in black churches for nearly his entire life. He has preached as an evangelist in Africa, Europe, and Canada, and all over the United States. He was in line to take over his uncle's church before, as he puts it, "this whole gay thing popped up." He began to struggle with the question of whether people would worship under an openly gay pastor.

At the same time, Clay started to work in organizations that addressed AIDS in the black community. That work brought him face-to-face with African-American gay men who were open about their sexuality. Ministering to them helped Clay along the journey to self-acceptance. He still works in AIDS prevention, most recently as a counselor and tester with the AIDS Survival Project in Atlanta. At Morehouse, Clay is active in another group he cofounded, Safe Space, which promotes equality and support for same-gender-loving men at the school.

Rashad's involvement with AIDS issues started in college and has become his life's work. He remembers a funeral he attended as a freshman for a family friend who had died of AIDS. During the eulogy, the preacher mentioned the deceased's involvement in a group having to do with A-I-D-S. He never spoke the word but instead spelled out the acronym one letter at a time, as if it were something else.

The symbolism of the preacher's reluctance to speak the word AIDS aloud was not lost on Rashad. He had been watching gay African-American men disappear before his eyes, yet no one was talking about it openly. The ranks of gospel choirs were thinning. Men would arrive with their skin and hair showing the ravages of AZT treatment, and still no one talked about the plague in their midst.

During the summer between his freshman and sophomore years at the University of Chicago, Rashad began to research AIDS and the response of the black church. It was partly an academic pursuit, but Rashad, like Clay, was beginning the process of reconciling his sexuality with his spirituality. The next summer, he researched the same topic from the perspective of people living with AIDS and HIV. He went on to get his master's degree in social science from the University of Chicago and moved into community work.

In Chicago, Rashad worked for the Howard Brown Health Centers and assisted the Chicago Department of Public Health in creating neighborhood HIV-prevention programs for African-American and Latino gay men. He helped cofound MOCHA, a coalition of community agencies working in AIDS prevention in Chicago's minority communities. With the success of locally focused projects under his belt, Rashad set his sights on national AIDS work and was hired by the CDC.

In his capacity as a team leader of seven project officers at the CDC, Rashad frequently travels around the country. He's struggling with how to balance his professional commitment with his work with Clay and The Vision Church. "The ministry is a further extension of the work I do. It's very much a divine calling—what I was created to do," he explains.

For Clay, his spiritual life—at least for now—is also a political one. "The simple act of being an openly gay man married to my partner makes my presence political," Clay says.

While that might be true for any gay pastor, Clay's racial identity is another factor. Black churches—like so many churches—have traditionally resisted recognizing or accepting homosexuality and there are concerns within the African-American community about the state of black masculinity. With staggering numbers of African-American men in prisons or unemployed, some see homosexuality as just another threat to the position of black men in African-American families.

Despite that pressure, Clay and Rashad don't want to go into hiding. On the contrary, they want their story, their lives, and their new church to help others who are struggling. "It's a holistic ministry. We'll empower people spiritually, educationally, and politically," says Clay. "The Vision Church is not a place where people have to check their brains at the door." And of course, they don't have to check their sexuality at the door either.

AIDS work and the church brought Clay and Rashad together. But it was hardly a direct path from first sight to wedded bliss. The two men met fleetingly in Chicago in 1999 at an Adodi conference, a spiritual retreat for African-American gay and bisexual men. They ran into each other again in Chicago five months later. And in 2002, they spied each other at the Tabernacle Baptist Church in Atlanta, the city that is to African-American gay men what San Francisco is for white gay men.

Clay laughs as he remembers his first impression of Rashad. "I'd heard about this great guy from Chicago doing great stuff with AIDS prevention. I was standing in the back of a conference hall and I saw Rashad. He was so beautiful." Later that day, Clay got a closer look when he stepped off an elevator and saw Rashad surrounded by a circle of admirers. They made eye contact. Rashad called to Clay, "Hey you—the cute one!" Put off by what he saw as Rashad's unabashed arrogance, Clay kept right on walking, partly annoyed, partly playing hard to get.

Five months later Clay was in Chicago again, visiting a friend from the Adodi conference, and ran into Rashad at a dance club. The energy between them was palpable, even though no words were exchanged. Rashad danced over to Clay, planted a passionate, I-want-to-go-to-bed-with-you kiss on his lips, and walked away. Once again, Clay was attracted and irritated by Rashad's combination of charm and conceit.

Coincidence brought them together again three years later. Rashad had taken a job at the CDC and Clay had enrolled at Morehouse, so both were now living in Atlanta. They both found their way to the Tabernacle Baptist Church, which advertised itself on the radio as a place of "love and acceptance." It took three consecutive Sundays of spotting each other at Tabernacle before they spoke, exchanged phone numbers, and began talking on the phone, for longer and longer each time. They arranged to go out to dinner after church one Sunday and fell in love.

Their first meal together lasted five hours. Rashad recalls getting up between courses to wash his hands in the bathroom. "I looked at myself in the mirror and said, 'This is it.'"

Back at the table, Clay was thinking, "My God. I could spend the rest of my life with this man." At the same time, he didn't know how that could happen. "Do gay people do that?" he wondered. He had no role models to tell him, "Yes, they do."

Clay and Rashad have now become those role models. They're married men, homeowners, and accomplished professionals. Sitting together on an overstuffed couch in their modern living room, they look back over the journey of their relationship with a giddy excitement that makes them seem like newlyweds. Leafing through the photo album of their wedding, Rashad's leg overlaps Clay's and Clay plays lovingly with Rashad's dreadlocks. They look back at the vows they read each other at sunrise and smile, delighted that the promises they made are intact and the love they expressed still burns.

"People still ask me why I *married* a man," says Clay. He'll be preaching his answer from the pulpit of his church for years to come: "I did it because I'm a Christian, and I believe in covenants and commitments."

Anne and Heather

*"Are they going to take Mommy
out of our family?"*

No topic of conversation is off-limits in the back seat of
Anne Magro's and Heather Finstuen's minivan. On some
days, their twin six-year-old daughters deconstruct beer advertising, trying to decipher why pictures of women in bathing suits
make people want to buy beer. Other days, they ponder whether
the people who don't want to live next to Native Americans are the
same ones who don't want to live next to African-Americans.

Their discussions aren't always so heavy. Sarah also likes to tout
the merits of the University of Michigan football team. And Kate
explains how her favorite Food Channel chef, Rachael Ray, has it
all over the more celebrated Emeril.

But the conversation their mother Anne remembers most acutely
was about George W. Bush. Driving home one summer evening in
2004, the family listened attentively to National Public Radio as
President Bush accepted the Republican Party's presidential nomi-
nation. "Our society rests on a foundation of responsibility and
character and family commitment," Bush said, his Texas accent
filling the otherwise silent minivan. "Because the union of a man
and woman deserves an honored place in our society, I support
the protection of marriage against activist judges." A campaign

stump speech is usually lost on kindergartners, but Kate listened intently—until the president's words were drowned out by her own sobbing. By the time they reached home, Kate was crying inconsolably. Anne carried her into her bedroom and patiently rubbed the little girl's back, waiting for the tears to subside.

At last, Kate was calm enough to speak. "If Bush is elected president," she asked, wiping away tears, "are they going to take Mommy out of our family?"

Anne, who is also Kate's mother, drew in a deep breath. "Mommy is your mom, and nobody can change that," she told Kate. "Being somebody's mom isn't something that the law can decide." Anne also explained to Kate and her sister Sarah, once again, that they were fighting a lawsuit in the courts to make sure that no one would ever take Mommy away from their family.

Anne and Heather are plaintiffs in a lawsuit that is seeking to overturn an Oklahoma law that says the state will not recognize as legal any adoptions entered into by same-sex parents in other states. After Anne gave birth to their twins in New Jersey in 1998,

Kate, Anne, Heather and Sarah

Heather adopted them and became their legal parent. When that adoption was finalized in 2000, Anne and Heather considered the matter settled. But after they moved to Oklahoma, the state legislature passed a law in 2004 that put Heather's status as one of the twins' parents at risk. Without legal status as a parent in Oklahoma, Heather could be prevented from doing many of the things parents routinely do for their children, such as registering them for school, visiting a sick child in the hospital, making health care decisions, or carrying children's health insurance. And there was the painful issue of who the children's legal guardian would be if Anne were to die.

Anne and Heather weighed carefully the decision to join the lawsuit that would thrust their young family into the spotlight of gay rights in the socially and religiously conservative environment of Oklahoma. But they quickly decided that the risks were worth it and that they were in a particularly good position to be the public face for their issue. "We're very lucky, because we both have families that love us, and we're not worried we're going to lose our jobs over this," says Anne. "We feel very privileged, and we have a comfortable lifestyle, surrounded by people who support us."

And the risks of not joining the lawsuit seemed too great. "We want to protect our kids and give them security and to give ourselves peace of mind—that if something unexpected were to happen everything is in place," says Heather. They have amassed piles of documents and paperwork outlining their life insurance policies and guardianship plans for Kate and Sarah, but legally and emotionally, those contingency plans fall short of the full status of parenthood. "Kids who have two legal parents who are committed to taking care of them are better off than those who don't," says Anne.

Oklahoma is the only state in the country that doesn't recognize the legality of a same-sex adoption established in another state. During debate over the new law, one senator commented that the statute was necessary because "the key component of the radical homosexual agenda is to take away the right of states to regulate and define adoptions, just as they are trying to redefine marriage across the nation." The legality of the Oklahoma law is certainly open to question. The U.S. Constitution's Full Faith and Credit Clause requires any state to recognize the legal relationships created under the laws of another state. The legal battle is certain to be long and emotional. And in the meantime, Heather has no legal rights as a parent.

"Every other state in the country would recognize the adoption," says Anne. "My initial reaction to this law was to tell Heather that if I died, the first thing she should do is take the kids and leave Oklahoma. But then I realized that was not the way to address the problem."

Anne and Heather are a high-achieving power couple. Heather, thirty-six, has a master's degree in anthropology and has traveled often on scientific expeditions to Ecuador. She gained a mastery of Spanish on these South American forays and put it to use as an editor of college foreign-language textbooks. After they moved to Oklahoma, Heather realized her true ambition was to be a lawyer, and she started law school at the University of Oklahoma two years ago, at the age of thirty-four. She's been a standout law student, rising to the sought-after position of editor in chief of the law review.

Anne, age forty-one, is on the faculty at the University of Oklahoma as an assistant professor of accounting in the College of Business. She was recruited while she was teaching at Rutgers University in New Jersey. As she awaits news of their lawsuit, she's also waiting for a decision about whether she will receive tenure.

Together for fourteen years, both women are intellectually sharp and extremely well-spoken. They are also quick to break into broad smiles and frequent bouts of infectious laughter. Despite the discriminatory law that is front and center in their family life, they both retain the optimism that has shaped their outlook.

"We were worried before the lawsuit that people would start stalking us or our children," says Anne. "But if you're not the kind of person who can imagine doing something really crazy to someone else, it's hard to imagine anyone else doing it to you. I couldn't imagine calling someone up and threatening their life, so it's hard to assess the likelihood that that would happen." And, in fact, it hasn't.

Heather's studies in law school give her hope about their chances of winning the civil law suit. "Law school has given me a new filter in interpreting the world, how it works, and how the law exists for everyone," she says, sounding very much like a lawyer. "The law is a public good. Whereas a political process that is driven by a majority can serve to strip people of civil rights, the law and our Constitution exist to protect against majority politics."

When Anne was being recruited for a job in the Sooner State, she and Heather took time to consider whether they wanted to move there. Oklahoma is known for its conservative Christian politics, and the couple wondered how their family would be received. Heather had never lived in that part of the country before. She was born and raised in Long Beach, California, where her parents still live in her childhood home. Anne had lived in Michigan and Ohio. For both of them, Oklahoma was uncharted territory for their family, which was sure to stand out in a "red" state.

"We never saw ourselves living in Oklahoma," Anne says. "But we really loved the school and the faculty. We came in with very low expectations, but we've been really happy here."

Norman, Oklahoma, is a college town with a population of one hundred thousand. Its high concentration of faculty with advanced degrees and students makes it a liberal pocket—maybe not compared to Berkeley or Cambridge, but certainly relative to the rest of the state. During her initial interview at the university, Anne told the faculty that she was interested in the position but that it would be a hard sell for her family. So the school arranged for Heather, Kate, and Sarah to fly out to see Norman for themselves.

The twins were just eighteen months old then, but the family toured elementary schools, met with principals, and visited daycare centers. All the while, Anne recalls, they were "very out." "We went to Wal-Mart and called each other "honey" and "sweetie" to see how people would react. Nobody said a thing and nobody looked at us funny. Either nobody was paying attention or nobody cared."

They began to feel comfortable and imagine that living in Norman might be possible for them. An unexpected encounter with a biker at a gas station helped them to make their decision. During a long car ride, Sarah had gotten sick and Anne pulled into a gas station. The attendant, wearing a leather vest and covered in tattoos rather than a shirt, quickly assessed the situation and brought out rolls of paper towels, a bucket of water, and trash bags. He helped Anne and Heather clean out the car. "Coming from New Jersey, seeing a biker ready to clean up the vomit was a good sign to me," Anne says.

Anne and Heather haven't found a large community of same-sex-headed families in Norman like the one they were part of in New Jersey. They did find and join the OKC Lesbian Moms, a small but steady group with about fifteen active member families who get together once a month for potlucks and kid-free outings for the parents. Very few families in Oklahoma were started with artificial insemination—as Anne's and Heather's was—or with adoption. They've found that most of the Oklahoma lesbians they know have their children from a previous marriage to a man. Anne and Heather now know a growing number of lesbian couples in Oklahoma who are exploring artificial insemination, but state laws don't make it easy for both members of theses couples to be legal parents. Not only does Oklahoma refuse to recognize same-sex adoptions from other states, Oklahoma forbids same-sex, second-parent adoptions for its residents as well.

Anne and Heather jokingly call themselves "the poster family for Lambda Legal," the national organization that promotes equal civil rights for lesbians, gay men, bisexual people, and transgender people and is representing them in the adoption lawsuit. Their talkative twin daughters show every indication at six years old that they'll grow up to be as bright and accomplished as their mothers. Intelligence sparkles in Kate's round brown eyes and in Sarah's hazel ones.

It's hard for Anne and Heather not to feel that they are constantly on display and that they need to be on their best behavior in public. They even feel pressure to have a well-tended lawn and garden. They are active participants in Kate's and Sarah's lives—carefully selecting a private school, limiting their television viewing, and engaging them in high-level conversations about any topic the girls see fit to raise.

Heather's schedule has been jam-packed with her law school classes, but she carves out time each night for family dinners—sometimes picnics on the law school campus. And no matter what, Saturday nights are Family Night. That usually means a dinner of appetizers —the twins' favorite meal—and an evening of kid-centered fun.

With Heather in law school, Anne's schedule allows more room for day-to-day activities with the girls. She coaches their soccer and T-ball teams and leads their Girl Scout troop. "I always knew I wanted to be a soccer coach, even before I had kids," Anne says.

She and Heather contemplated kids for a long time before they had them. They had been together for six years when they decided Anne would begin undergoing artificial insemination. Her doctor prescribed the treatment and recommended that Anne's insurance cover it. Without batting an eye, the doctor wrote on the form that Anne's partner was unable to produce sperm.

For thirteen frustrating months, Anne underwent artificial insemination procedures with no success. At last, after several different types of treatment and megadoses of vitamin B, Anne got pregnant. During a sonogram at eight weeks of pregnancy, a doctor asked Anne and Heather if they had considered the risks of undergoing certain tests when carrying twins.

"Why did you say that?" Anne asked.

"Because you're having twins," the doctor said.

"How do you know?" challenged Heather.

"Two heartbeats."

Anne lay on the examining table and laughed. Twins! The doctor advised them that many twins don't survive at that stage of pregnancy, so they should think carefully before telling people—advice Heather took to heart. Anne, however, did not. That night they went out to dinner to celebrate. When the server politely asked, "How are you?" Anne blurted out, "I'm having twins!"

Living in Oklahoma, Anne and Heather are often the first openly gay family that many people they come in contact with have ever met. In her close-knit law school class of 180 students, Heather has felt like an ambassador for the cause. She hasn't found a lot of diversity of sexual orientation in her class or experience among her classmates in meeting "out" gay people. But she's felt warm acceptance from her fellow students, who have come to know Anne, Kate, and Sarah for the loving family they are. "Anne and I have gotten a lot of support on campus," says Heather, particularly after word spread of the anti-gay adoption law that was passed at the end of her first year of law school. "Students were coming up to me saying, 'This law is crazy! Your family is so nice and your kids are wonderful.'" Since Heather and Anne joined the lawsuit, several of her law professors have approached Heather with offers of help and strategic legal advice.

"There are probably people in my class who are not supportive, but they don't say anything," says Heather. "I have to approach the issue gingerly because it has the possibility of being divisive, politics being what they are." The start of her second year of law school saw the reelection of George W. Bush, who captured the vote of 66 percent of Oklahomans. Seventy-six percent of Oklahoma voters cast their ballot in 2004 in favor of a state constitutional amendment defining marriage as the union of a man and a woman. The measure also declared that only married people are eligible for the benefits of marriage and that same-sex marriages from other states are not valid in Oklahoma.

"I'm not in law school to debate my personal life or to thrust my beliefs on anyone," says Heather calmly. "But if people want to talk about it, I'll tell them what I think. My approach has been to lead by example and earn people's respect through my personality and by letting them see my commitment to my family. That's a much better way of gaining people's friendship and allegiance than through dogma."

Her approach has been yielding results, one person at a time. "We've had a lot of positive experiences with people one-on-one," says Anne, recounting a tearful undergraduate student who praised her family effusively. Heather, Anne, and the girls spent seven weeks in England while Heather attended an Oklahoma College of Law summer program at Oxford University between her first and second years. At the end of the summer, another student—a quintessential Oklahoma fraternity boy, complete with backwards-turned baseball cap—told Anne and Heather what a tremendous experience it had been for him to get to know their family. "I was raised to believe that what you are doing is wrong," he told them. "But I don't know how anybody could know your family and believe that." Anne and Heather, he said, were role models as parents.

Academic environments have been home to Anne and Heather as long as they have known each other. They met at the University of Illinois at Urbana-Champaign when Heather was twenty-three and pursing a doctorate in anthropology and Anne was twenty-seven, working on her doctorate in accounting.

Heather was attracted to Anne's intelligence, generosity, and sense of humor, and Anne valued the same qualities in Heather. They met at the end of April, just as the school year was drawing to a close. Heather was flying back to California for the summer, and she and Anne had a hurried good-bye. "Heather gave me a peck on the lips and took off. I was totally unprepared and didn't even kiss back," Anne recalls, still regretting her failure to reciprocate.

But the summer was not a loss. Conspiring with a friend of Heather's in Los Angeles, Anne arranged to fly to California to surprise Heather for her birthday. Heather had been growing increasingly disgruntled at the lack of plans to recognize her twenty-fourth birthday. She complained to Anne that her friend Sheila was insisting that she drive to the airport on her birthday to pick up a friend she didn't even know. Much to Heather's surprise, she found Anne waiting on the curb at the airport instead. "She was so flustered, she couldn't unlock the car to get out," Anne says, laughing.

Back in Champaign, the relationship between the two women grew over the next year, and the following summer they moved in together in a house Anne owned with her brother Bill. They shared the house with Bill and his wife, Lisa, until Lisa became pregnant. Anne and Heather got a house of their own, where they lived until moving to New Jersey for Anne's teaching position at Rutgers.

As they settled into New Jersey life, Anne and Heather began to regret that they hadn't held a commitment ceremony with their friends and family in Illinois before they left. Here in this new place, they knew almost no one. In their own hearts, however, they knew their deep commitment to each other, and they both wore rings that they had exchanged privately.

"We bought a house and got a thirty-year mortgage. That makes you feel very connected to somebody," says Heather. Then they had their children and went through Heather's adoption process. "Our connection is built on a promise. It's just not a promise we made publicly."

They watched carefully as Massachusetts legalized gay marriage and skeptically as civil unions were created in Vermont and Connecticut. "There's a big misconception that civil unions are the same thing as marriage," says Heather. "People don't realize that civil unions are just local and that they don't give full benefits."

Federal benefits, including social security benefits and the ability to file joint tax returns, are the grand prize for which Anne and Heather are holding out. While they devote their time and emotional resources to fighting for same-sex adoption rights in Oklahoma, they've resolved to wait until same-sex marriage is embraced nationally before they walk down the aisle together: "We've decided that we're going to wait for the whole enchilada," says Heather.

They're both optimistic that legalized same-sex marriage will become a reality in their lifetimes. "I think we'll get there before we die, as long as we live a long time," says Heather, with the hopefulness that is a hallmark of both their personalities. "I'd love it to happen right now, but these things happen slowly. When we think about history and courts and laws and how long it takes for culture to change, it takes a long time. Slavery ended in the mid- to late-1800s, and we didn't have desegregation and civil rights until a hundred years later."

As much as laws will help, Heather believes that personal transformations matter at least as much. "There's a huge generational divide" in acceptance of gay marriage, she says. "But today more people know of a gay relative. Our stories are starting to make sense."

In her own family, Heather has presented a learning opportunity for her parents and even her eighty-six-year-old grandmother, who is a supportive great-grandmother to Kate and Sarah. Heather came out to her parents in graduate school. She remembers their shock and many questions about all the boys she had dated and whether she was really sure she was a lesbian. But even during her first discussions with her parents, Heather felt assured of their unconditional love.

Heather's parents have grown more accepting and supportive as time has gone on, particularly since they've become grandparents. Despite their initial reservations fourteen years ago, Heather's parents now find themselves writing letters to the governor of Oklahoma, advocating for gay rights and imploring him not to pass a regressive law that penalizes same-sex parents. Like Anne's parents in Ohio, Heather's make regular visits to Oklahoma to see their grandchildren, and holidays are always a family affair.

"When you have children, you force your parents to 'come out,'" says Heather, noting that her parents are so excited about their grandchildren that they want to share their news with other people. "Both of our sets of parents have really risen to the occasion and are very supportive of us."

Loving relationships with their families of origin bring Anne and Heather no small measure of peace—especially since Heather's parental rights are open to question in Oklahoma. "One thing that gay families think about a lot is if something happens to me, is my family going to respect my partner and allow her to make decisions? Especially when there are children. If something were to happen to Anne, I could envision a very scary custody dispute if I don't have legal protections."

Anne and Heather have designated their former roommates from years ago, Anne's brother Bill and his wife, Lisa, as guardians of Kate and Sarah. "We know they would never contest my legal ties as a parent," says Heather. "We trust them totally."

Anne and Heather have diligently made all their worst-case-scenario plans. But their primary focus is day-to-day life with two bright and inquisitive six-year-olds. Even when they're consumed by details surrounding their lawsuit, their more pressing concerns are about what's for dinner. "We try to stress that we are just parents, and we have all the same concerns that all good parents have," says Anne. "We worry about our kids being safe and healthy and who's going to pick the kids up from soccer. We're just regular people."

The whole family finds life in the spotlight overwhelming at times, and they have the same long to-do lists as any other couple with young children. "Sometimes it's tiring," Anne admits. "But it's hard to distinguish how much is being tired of being an ambassador and how much is just being tired."

Sarah hasn't shown any signs that she is exhausted by the push for her family's rights. But Anne and Heather have heard Kate complain that she is tired of their family being in the news. They've never shielded the twins from the issues. Anne and Heather have made every effort to explain the issues to the girls at a level they can understand. It would be nearly impossible to hide their mothers' advocacy. The family has talked to reporters and appeared on television. And the girls—both early readers—have spotted articles about the family in newspapers left on the dining room table. "Some people tell me that I tell my kids too much," says Anne, unapologetically adding, "I talk to them like adults. I try not to tell them more than they are asking, but I don't ever feel like I should not tell."

Sarah and Kate are finding that notoriety can have its privileges. The family has been asked to serve as the grand marshals of the 2005 Oklahoma City Gay Pride Day parade. There will be balloons, Mardi Gras beads, and with luck, plenty of candy. It's a wonderful gesture of welcome for the whole family and shows that they can be loved and celebrated in Oklahoma.

There are many days when Anne and Heather wonder if they should pack up and find a more accepting community in which to raise their daughters. "There are some arguments for leaving," says Anne. "If we can't get the law off the books that says Heather is not Kate and Sarah's parent, we won't stay in Oklahoma, because it puts our kids at risk."

Wherever they go, Anne and Heather are aware that they'll be trailblazers in a world where lesbian-headed families are targets of discrimination—at least for now. Ever hopeful, they believe that hatred toward gay people will dissipate. But Heather allows some frustration to mix with her optimism. "I see some of our country's problems in terms of the economy and the war in Iraq and the perception of our country in the world, but what conservative politicians are focusing on is this 'scary gay marriage.' I can't help but conclude that their opposition is disingenuous and political—a way to rally people to support them based on their divisive ignorance."

The Oklahoma law that won't recognize her parenting rights is particularly divisive and profligate, Heather asserts. "It's a waste of time and money to pass laws that are unconstitutional. The taxpayers wind up footing the bill for all the time and money it takes to have it struck down. It's an irresponsible use of public resources."

Whether Anne and Heather stay in Oklahoma will depend on whether those public resources lead to more rights for their family or less. In the meantime, Anne and Heather and Kate and Sarah are keeping their options open.

Gary and Rich

"You and Dad are married, right?"

When Paige Chalmers got the phone call from her dads that gay marriage was becoming legal in Massachusetts, her reaction was succinct, enthusiastic, and loud.

"Yippee!" she yelled into the phone, jumping up and down with her best friend, Danyelle. That call instantly changed November 18, 2003, from an ordinary day in sixth grade to a historic moment for Paige's family and for gay and lesbian couples across the country. But it wasn't equity for same-sex couples that had Paige celebrating. She was thrilled that she'd soon be planning a wedding.

Other than the impending wedding—with its promises of dancing, dressing up, and a rare opportunity to wear makeup—Paige wasn't looking into the future and seeing a different life. She'd lived with Daddy Gary and Daddy Rich for all of her eleven years. To her, it had never felt like a bold social experiment or an alternative family. Gary Chalmers and Richard Linnell were simply her loving parents, her chauffeurs to dance class or horseback riding, and the doting dads who tucked her in at night.

Until she was eight, Paige didn't even know that her parents weren't married. But an argument with her ten-year-old cousin changed that, in a moment as starkly shocking as when a child first learns that Santa Claus isn't real. Her cousin had been vehemently insisting that a marriage could only be between a man and a woman. Paige argued back just as forcefully that men could be married, too. She sought out Gary so he could confirm what she already knew to be true.

"You and Dad are married, right?" she asked. Gary had to admit that, in fact, they were not.

As transforming as this knowledge was for Paige, it was equally jarring to Gary and Rich. "We realized then that we shouldn't have to explain to our daughter that her parents aren't married. We knew we had to get involved in trying to change the law."

So in April of 2001, Gary and Rich went together to the clerk's office in the bucolic central Massachusetts town of Northridge to apply for a marriage license. A town of 14,500 people, Northridge is a suburb of Worcester dotted with farms, hay fields, and stone walls. It's the town where Rich was born and raised in the same house where Gary and Rich are now raising Paige. After their request for a marriage license was denied, they joined six other Massachusetts couples to file the now-famous lawsuit *Goodridge et al. v. the Massachusetts Department of Public Health.*

Paige is a lanky colt of a girl with long, straight chestnut hair, a shy smile, and round brown eyes. At twelve, she's caught somewhere between girlhood and womanhood. Her room is filled with posters of horses, kittens, and Britney Spears along with the high heels and makeup she loves to wear for special occasions. She likes to listen to music, watch television, hang out with friends, and talk about boys.

She dreams of one day getting a horse—a goal she's closing in on by working at the local stable where she takes riding lessons. "First I have to show that I can take care of my cats," Paige says. Once she proves she can tend to Pumpkin and Alexis, she's hoping a horse won't be far behind.

Paige's childhood appears idyllic, unfolding in a spacious house with a barn and pool out back. Rolling in the driveway are soccer balls, a basketball, and a football that she tosses with a tight spiral. Paige seems innocently unaware of the trailblazing her fathers have done, and she's only recently become aware of the vitriol that has sometimes been directed at them.

Gary and Rich have purposefully sheltered Paige from much of the hateful speech that is hurled at gays and lesbians generally and at Gary and Rich specifically as the lawsuit progressed through the courts. But as the day of the decision grew closer and media coverage increased, they gradually began to allow Paige to watch some protests on the evening news.

"We've tried to keep her out of the spotlight," says Gary. As Paige has gotten older, however, her parents have slowly revealed more layers of the issue to her. She was only eight when they filed their lawsuit. But by the time she turned eleven, Rich and Gary were letting her watch some of the interviews they gave to television reporters. Typically, these reports came with an opposing view, which gave Paige her first glimpse at anti-gay activism and rhetoric, complete with predictions that gays would burn in hell.

Paige seems unfazed by such criticism and she displays a maturity beyond her years. "It scares people because they're scared of something different," she says of the critics. She has rarely come

Rich, Paige and Gary

face-to-face with such ill will. Her friends have all been supportive and excited.

After the Goodridge decision came down from the Massachusetts Supreme Judicial Court, Gary and Rich decided that Paige could speak to reporters for the first time. It was a task she relished and her friends admired. "They all thought it was great that I was on TV," she says, beaming at the notoriety it gave her among her peers. "I was a little more popular because of it."

It's not that Paige is overlooking her father's detractors. It's just that among the younger generations, there aren't many. "People under twenty just don't understand what the big deal is," says Gary. "For the younger generation, gay marriage is very matter-of-fact."

Whether the younger generation realizes it or not, the Goodridge decision was groundbreaking. In addition to being plaintiffs in this lawsuit, Gary and Richard were mentioned by name in it:

> Gary Chalmers and Richard Linnell alleged that Gary pays for a family health insurance policy at work which covers only him and their daughter because Massachusetts law does not consider Rich to be a "dependent." This means that their household must purchase a separate individual policy of health insurance for Rich at considerable expense. . . . Gary has a pension plan at work, but under state law, because he is a municipal employee, that plan does not allow him the same range of options in providing for his beneficiary that a married spouse had and thus cannot provide the same security to his family that a married person could if he should predecease Rich.

The Massachusetts Supreme Judicial court found that "the marriage ban works deep and scarring hardship on a very real segment of the community for no rational reason." The court went on to say,

> Because [marriage] fulfills yearnings for security, safe haven, and connection that express our common humanity, civil marriage is an esteemed institution, and the decision whether and whom to marry is among life's momentous acts of self-definition. Therefore,

without the right to choose to marry, same-sex couples are not only denied full protection of the laws, but are excluded from the full range of human experience.

"We declare," the court concluded, "that barring an individual from the protections, benefits, and obligations solely because that person would marry a person of the same sex violates the Massachusetts Constitution." The court commanded the Massachusetts legislature to create a marriage law that would conform to its decision. When the legislature came back to the court a month later asking if it could create civil unions instead, the court said no. Anything short of full civil marriage, the court said, would create an "unconstitutional, inferior, and discriminatory status for same-sex couples."

Gary was ecstatic about the decision when it was handed down. "We are thrilled!" he said. "We've always been like every other family in our neighborhood. But now the one difference has been wiped away. When we get married, we and our daughter will be less vulnerable and more secure."

Gary and Rich adopted Paige at birth. They had been together for four years and were just beginning the process of exploring ways to adopt a child. At the same time, a family member put them in touch with an acquaintance in Maine—an eighteen-year-old who was pregnant with a baby she didn't feel she could raise. Gary and Rich reached an arrangement with the teenager to adopt her child. Twelve years later, it is still an open adoption, and Paige visits with her biological mother every eight weeks.

"We didn't know whether we were adopting a boy or a girl," recalls Rich. Both Gary and Rich have always surrounded Paige with many female role models. Rich's mother lives upstairs from the family and looks after Paige every day after school. Gary's parents and sister live just two miles away.

"And she knows which of us to go to for what," Rich, a registered nurse and nursing instructor, explains with a laugh. "She comes to me with her medical issues and goes to Gary for her school issues." Gary has been a schoolteacher in his nearby hometown of Shrewsbury for seventeen years. "I also go to Gary for soda," Paige chimes in. Rich doesn't let her drink it.

"Having two dads is all I've ever known." Paige's nonchalant shrug makes any question about whether having two fathers is a problem for her seem downright silly. Either she hasn't yet developed the knee-jerk embarrassment about expressing emotion that many teens have or she never will. "I love you both," she says, turning her head quickly from one side to the other to smile at both dads. Sitting barefoot on the couch next to Gary, she holds his hand while she talks, absentmindedly playing with his fingers as if they were her own.

Paige recalls a few books from her early childhood that emphasized two-father families, and she smiles remembering her favorite, *One Dad, Two Dads, Brown Dad, Blue Dads*. With her kindergarten teacher's encouragement, Paige even shared the book with the other five-year-olds in her first year of school.

"We've touched base with Paige's teachers through this whole process to make sure things were fine in school," says Gary. "Kids don't always tell you the whole story." Paige's teachers have been consistently supportive of her, and they've agreed that her peers have been unruffled by her family arrangement. The kids were interested in Paige's television appearances. And like Paige, they wanted to know when the wedding would be.

Luckily for Paige, there were two weddings.

On May 17, the day same-sex marriage became legal in Massachusetts, Gary and Rich marched up the steps of Worcester City Hall to once again apply for a marriage license. This time they got it, and they marched back down the steps with a license in hand, cheered on by the hundreds of supporters surrounding City Hall who had gathered to witness and applaud history.

They applied for a waiver to suspend the typical three-day waiting period for marriages and were married in a simple small ceremony at the Unitarian Universalist Church of Worcester. Along with an intimate group of close friends and family, Paige was there, wearing makeup, in a flowered lavender sun dress and high heels.

Four months later, Paige got the wedding she'd been waiting for. September 11, 2004, marked the sixteenth anniversary of Gary and Rich's relationship. They were already legally married, so they crafted a ceremony that blessed their vows, followed by a 230-person blowout celebration. The guests' ages spanned seventy-one years, with twelve-year-old Paige the youngest and her eighty-three-year-old great-aunt the oldest.

For Gary and Rich, it was a dream celebration of the rights for which they had battled for three long years. But it was also a chance to toast the friends and family who had loved and supported them along the way. "Those three years of the lawsuit were an incredible journey," says Gary. "I learned so much about our friends and family and the human spirit in general." And the party was a chance to honor them all for their support.

Gary recalls Mary Bonauto, the attorney with the Gay and Lesbian Advocates and Defenders who argued and won the Goodridge decision for equal marriage rights, telling them in the beginning stages of the lawsuit, "'We will fight the legal battles. You put a human face on it. You won't persuade the people on the far right. Go for the people on the fence.'"

For years, friends and relatives had contributed valuable public relations work for the cause just by discussing the case with their friends, families, and colleagues. They would come back to Gary and Rich and replay the debates they'd had, asking for advice on how to handle questions and issues the next time they came up. They created a circle of grassroots support around the family, and that unconditional encouragement was toasted all night long during the wedding celebration.

"We danced all night!" says Paige, beaming as she recalls the party. In Worcester's elegantly restored Mechanic's Hall, a DJ spun all of Paige's favorites, from the old, Donna Summer and Celine Dion, to the new, Britney Spears and the Backstreet Boys. Allowed to choose one guest of her own for the evening, Paige picked Danyelle, who had been beside her months before when Paige received the call from her fathers that they would, in fact, be married. Paige wore a beautiful dress for the occasion—deep purple with a halter top. And she learned that even though it's fun to wear high heels, the best thing is kicking them off to dance all night.

Mandy and Angela

"There's no mold for us to follow."

Big things seem to happen to Mandy and Angela around the holidays. Their first date was on the Fourth of July. Basic training began for Angela on Valentine's Day. On one Christmas, Angela proposed to Mandy. On another Christmas, Mandy's father died.

Mandy and Angela are a wholesome-looking, earnest young couple. In their late twenties, they have already been together for seven years, building a life in what looks like the most inhospitable of circumstances. They live in the heart of the Bible Belt, and they've both chosen careers that are unwelcoming to lesbians. Yet their striking brand of optimism has helped them navigate with good humor what many people might see as insurmountable obstacles. Mandy and Angela have remained in the heartland, shrugging off the daily discriminations they encounter. They are rebels with a cause, engaged in small, everyday insurrections.

"We're dancing without music right now," says Angela, a wiry twenty-eight-year-old with tousled brown hair. "We're two lesbians who got married barefoot in the park. It's not like we aren't going to meet anyone's expectations. There's no mold for us to follow."

They've drawn strength from each other and from the communities they've carefully constructed, first in Oklahoma City and then in Kansas City, Missouri, where they live now. Where they'll go next, they have no idea, as they continue to cut their own paths.

Mandy is a seminary student at Saint Paul School of Theology, affiliated with the United Methodist Church. "United Methodists won't ordain anyone who is a self-avowed, practicing homosexual," says Mandy, stringing together the words with the ease of someone who's said them enough times that they don't seem to hurt her anymore. But that doesn't mean she's in hiding or will go into hiding to seek ordination. Instead, she's planning to pursue a lay position in a Methodist movement with a long-standing activist tradition.

Angela, however, has had to hide. She's a member of the Air National Guard, and the U.S. military's "Don't Ask, Don't Tell" policy has forced her to keep her relationship with Mandy private. (And that is why, in this chapter, no last names are used.) Angela never anticipated that the Guard would occupy so much of her life. But she completed her training in September 2001, just a few weeks after the September 11 attacks and has been deployed on military missions three times so far since then—flying on aeromedical

Angela and Mandy

evacuation missions in Afghanistan, Iraq, and Kuwait. She also had a tour of duty based in Washington, D.C., escorting injured soldiers back home or into military hospitals for long-term care.

"When I first joined the squadron and social situations would come up, it got harder and harder to be quiet and ambiguous about my personal life," says Angela. "But I've been in the military long enough to find safe people." In addition, she finds that the military in general tends to attract lesbians, and the medical units, in particular, attract gay male nurses. She's surrounded by people keeping their sexuality secret from the military brass.

Mandy, the seminary student who can't be ordained as a Methodist minister, is clearly in love with Angela, a Methodist-Buddhist soldier serving in the Iraq war as a conscientious objector. With so many dissonant chords in their professional lives, it's a comfort in the evening to come home and simply be together.

The couple has always gotten complete support from Angela's family. Mandy has endured years of skepticism from her family and still speaks to some relatives only rarely. The toughest conversion of all was her father, and Mandy didn't learn how totally he had accepted Angela until the day after he died.

Angela is a country girl, born in Kansas and bred in Oklahoma. Mandy grew up in various parts of the country as her engineer parents moved around to Florida, Michigan, and New Jersey, where she attended high school. The two women wove their worlds together at their wedding ceremony in September 1999 in Oklahoma City.

They had been college sweethearts. They met in their dorm at Oklahoma City University, a Methodist school. It was a familiar setting for Angela, who had grown up in Christian youth groups, church drama clubs, and choirs. But during Angela's college years, Buddhism began to supplant Christianity in her mind.

As Angela moved toward Eastern thought, Mandy was discovering the Methodist religion for the first time. She had come to OCU for its opera and musical theater programs, not its dogma. The Methodist world was a mystery and a surprise. "Growing up all my friends were either Catholics or Jews," says Mandy. "I was in culture shock. Here I was in the Bible Belt, in the Midwest. There were one Jew and three Catholics on campus." Mandy had been raised Catholic but never felt comfortable in the tradition. She remembers telling her parents as a child that the Church's rules didn't make sense to her. "They didn't make sense to my parents, either, but they liked the traditions," says Mandy.

Mandy started attending a Methodist church with her friends and felt comfortable and interested. The Church was grabbing her at the same time that operatic training was losing its appeal. Before meeting Angela, Mandy had dated a few men in what she describes as short, unhealthy relationships. Angela, on the other hand, had fallen into a pattern of dating women who were dating women for the first time. So they both entered the relationship with caution. But caution gave way to irresistible attraction. Conversations grew longer, stretching late into the night, and soon they were inseparable. They decided to try being roommates, and that sealed their desire to be a couple.

That's when they started seeing fireworks. Mandy and Angela had their first public date on the Fourth of July, 1997, wandering through the summer celebrations in Oklahoma City hand in hand. It was an exciting evening for Angela because her previous girlfriend had refused to show any affection to her in public. For Mandy, it was her first evening "out" as a lesbian. Mandy felt vaguely self-conscious and focused on watching people watching her. Most, she noticed, paid no attention. Some commented, "That's two women holding hands!" and then scurried away.

Their lives began to revolve more tightly around each other. By Christmastime, they were daunted by the idea of being away from each other for even that short break. Mandy was getting ready to fly home to New Jersey to spend the holidays with her parents. Angela didn't want her to leave without a symbol of her commitment to her lover. She bought two matching sterling bracelets. As she gave one to Mandy, Angela asked, "Would you like to marry me?"

"Yes," Mandy said. But that was quickly followed by "No! It doesn't work that way!"

Mandy recalls thinking at the time, "I just don't know what marriage would look like." Still, she boarded the plane back to New Jersey with a promise and a thrill of excitement. She was beaming when her parents greeted her. When Mandy told them about her newfound love, however, they didn't share her joy.

"It's a phase," they insisted. Mandy's parents expressed a deep concern for Angela, and they insisted Mandy must be leading her on. Surely Mandy would break Angela's heart when she came to her senses and left her for a man.

Driving back to the airport, Mandy's father began asking her how she was going to break up with Angela, helping her plan her exit strategy. She boarded the plane in haste and met Angela at the airport in tears. "I had to do a lot of soul-searching about how much Angela meant to me. I tried to make my family understand that this was not a lack of respect for them. I love Angela, and I hoped they could understand that one day."

Mandy's family did not respond with understanding. Instead they made Mandy swear that she wouldn't tell anyone else in the family.

Mandy kept that promise for about a year. But by the next Christmas, she and Angela were officially engaged to be married, and Mandy wanted to alert her cousins, aunts, grandparents, and uncles to save the date. As she wrote her Christmas cards, she enclosed a note announcing that she'd be marrying Angela the following fall and asking them to please save the date of September 25. A few relatives elected to send their regrets in advance of an official invitation. Her great-aunt wrote to say that Mandy would burn in hell. "Baby child?" she asked. "What are you thinking?"

As the date of the wedding approached, Mandy's family was firm in its resolve not to attend. Angela's family had the opposite reaction. Her mother, Janet, had already volunteered to sew wedding clothes for the brides and their attendants, who included Angela's sister, Lissa.

Angela came out to her family with no fanfare—much to her dismay. She had spent two months in San Diego the summer after her first year of college. Before she returned to Oklahoma, she was determined to tell her mother that she had a girlfriend and to ask for acceptance of who she really was. Angela wrote a long, emotional letter. One night she decided to call her mother and read it to her over the phone. From the nonchalance of her mother's reaction, Angela felt she might as well have been telling her that the weather was warm and sunny in Southern California.

"My mom said, 'I kind of knew that you were gay ever since you were a little kid,'" Angela recalls. "I ended up being the one who got mad. I asked, 'Well, then, why didn't you tell me?'"

But Angela's family didn't talk about those kinds of things. Indeed, Angela's mother's initial sex education from her own mother had been astoundingly brief. "Men and women just kind of fit together," Angela's grandmother had explained. When Angela was about nine, her mother had asked her now ex-husband, "Have you ever entertained the possibility that Angela is gay?" Angela's father was appalled. "I can't believe you'd say that about your own daughter," he said. They never discussed the matter again.

With the wedding pending in September, Mandy's parents met Angela for the first time when they flew down to Oklahoma City for Mandy's graduation ceremony in May 1999. Mandy's skeptical parents were accompanied by her skeptical brother, skeptical grandmother, and skeptical aunt and uncle. In a long-standing family tradition, Mandy prepared chicken cutlets and spaghetti.

Tensions were running high, but not as high as Mandy and Angela had expected. Just the week before, a band of lethal tornados had devastated Oklahoma City. Mandy had been working overtime as a 911 operator, fielding calls from people ravaged by the tornados' destructive force. Angela was toiling day and night with a volunteer search-and-rescue team, pulling survivors from the wreckage. In light of all this, entertaining homophobic parents was a luxury problem.

Conversation over chicken cutlets was civil and brief. Angela wolfed down dinner so she could hustle off to her job as an OCU security officer. "I was a walking stereotype," Angela says. She laughs as she recalls strapping on a bullet-proof vest and a gun after dinner, under the watchful eyes of Mandy's family.

The next day, Mandy's graduation, was a trying one for Angela. She had dropped out of school a few months earlier to pursue a career as an Emergency Medical Technician (EMT), while she continued to work for OCU. Working as a security officer, Angela was stationed on the floor of Mandy's graduation ceremony. Through all the pomp and circumstance she felt Mandy's entire family watching her. With each glance, the family seemed to strengthen their resolve not to attend the next ceremony, Mandy and Angela's wedding in September.

"My father was completely centered on his family," Mandy recalls, brushing back the shoulder-length, light-brown hair that frames the smooth skin of her round face. "If he had free time to spend, he felt he had to spend it with his family."

Mandy is convinced that her parents withheld their blessing on the wedding because they assumed Mandy and Angela couldn't have a wedding if family didn't show up. They had no idea how many friends and members of Angela's family were already planning to attend.

For a year and a half, the couple had been saving their money and honing the details of an elaborate ceremony, which would take place in Will Rogers Park. Angela's mother had finished Mandy's dress, a full-length, square-necked, champagne-satin gown. She'd also sewn a long, Asian-influenced, champagne-satin jacket for Angela to wear over peach satin pants. For the female attendants, she'd designed dresses; for the male attendants, she'd sewn ties. All the clothes were in the colors of the sunset, a fall palette for their outdoor wedding in a rose garden.

Mandy forged ahead with wedding plans, using her excitement for the ceremony to block out the pain of her parents' refusal to come. Back in New Jersey, they were focused on her brother, Tony, and his impending Thanksgiving-weekend wedding, a large formal affair, planned in grand Italian-American tradition.

Three weeks before Mandy's and Angela's wedding, sensing there was nothing they could do to stop the runaway train of the couple's resolve, Mandy's parents made a surprising announcement: They were coming to the wedding.

Mandy's mother, father, and brother flew in late the night before. The other twenty-five members of her family that Mandy had hopefully invited had all declined. The two families met for the first time at a wedding breakfast, hastily arranged at an International House of Pancakes restaurant. Just as tornados had distracted them from family drama at Mandy's graduation, the anticipation of the wedding kept Mandy and Angela from fretting over who was sitting next to whom and which future in-law was offending the other. Pancakes were served as Mandy and Angela briefed Mandy's family on where to stand and what to do.

The ceremony was an artful mix of Christianity and Buddhism. The minister of their Methodist church was forbidden by Methodist rules from performing the ceremony, so two friends in seminary school did the honors. To symbolize their connection to the earth, Mandy and Angela walked down the grassy aisle barefoot. Bemused, Mandy's father and Angela's stepfather took off their shoes as well to escort them down the aisle. "People thought it was so sweet and that they were doing it in solidarity," Mandy says, laughing. "But they were really mocking us!"

Angela vowed, "Mandy, I love you. I have spent the last few years of my life learning who I am and who you are. During that time I have experienced love and beauty more than I could ever imagine. I have decided that my life is best spent with you. I want to build, from mine and yours, one life together. I want to give to you the best of who I am and who I can be. I commit myself to you today and forever. I promise to work, play, and to dream with you. I will share and respect your dreams. I will make the joys and pains of your life my own and share my joys and pains with you. I promise to respect your needs and mine, even when that need is space. I promise to always continue learning about you and about myself. I will remind myself to see the beauty in our diversity. I promise to seek your forgiveness when we have forgotten respect for each other. I will go the journey with you."

Mandy vowed, "Of all the people I have known on my journey through life, it is you with whom I choose to journey in this covenant. With you and your life, I choose to weave the strands of mine. I love you, Angela, with all of my heart and all of my soul. I want to give you the best of who I am and who I am becoming. I know the journey won't be easy, but I also know that I live better when I live with you. I love you for who you are—not some ideal person I think you could be. I love your values, your passion, your spirituality, your caring and commitment to all people, your intelligence, your wonderful sense of humor, and of course, your beautiful eyes and incredible smile. I promise to work, play, and dream with you and to do my best to help those dreams come true. I promise to share your tears and laughter and to allow you to share mine. I promise to respect the need of both of us to have separate space and to come back to you as I trust you to come back to me. I celebrate our differences and rejoice in our love for always and forever."

A simple reception followed in the hall of the Methodist church for their seventy-five guests. "Church rules say only that we couldn't have the ceremony in the church," says Mandy. "They didn't say anything about the reception."

Angela nods, grinning. "We're continually looking for loopholes."

"Yes," agrees Mandy. "We're both always finding ways to make space for ourselves where we're not wanted."

Their brazen approach was beginning to affect Mandy's parents. Mandy sensed that they were astonished to see how many supporters they had, and it helped allay their fears that Mandy and Angela would be alienated in the world. At the reception, however, her parents' concern shifted to food. "I think they thought our wedding was a little rinky-dink," says Angela. The spread of hors d'oeuvres and wedding cake didn't jibe with their conviction that all weddings should include elaborate sit-down meals. After the reception Mandy's parents spontaneously proposed to all a dinner on them at the local Spaghetti Warehouse. "They felt guilty about not being involved, and they felt there needed to be a meal," says Mandy.

As Mandy and Angela headed off to San Antonio, Texas, for their honeymoon, Mandy's family returned to New Jersey, with the ice among them beginning to thaw. But it was a private peace. In public, Mandy's parents still expressed shame. The next family event, just two months later, was Tony's blowout wedding. Angela attended as Mandy's "friend." Family acquaintances teased Mandy about her little brother getting married first. Would she be following suit soon? In accordance with her parent's wishes, Mandy never told any of the nosy wedding guests that she was already married and accompanied by Angela, her bride.

It happened slowly, but Mandy's parents began to warm to Angela. The couple continued to spend most Christmases with Angela's family, which was a short drive away and more accepting. At Angela's house it was easier to ignore that back in New Jersey, all of Mandy's family members had stockings hanging on the mantel, their names written on them in glitter—all except for Angela. Even Tony's wife had gotten a stocking when she was still only his fiancée.

To help celebrate her mother's fiftieth birthday, Mandy's parents invited Mandy and Angela to accompany them on a ten-day Caribbean cruise. At breakfast each morning on the ship, Mandy's parents began to enjoy Angela's infectious sense of humor and storytelling flair. A little more than a year after the wedding, Mandy's parents invited Angela to call them "Mom" and "Dad."

Angela wasn't quite ready to take that step. Her hurt from years of being snubbed hadn't completely healed. But by Christmas of that year, 2001, she felt ready to call Mandy's parents by those intimate names. Mandy and Angela flew to New Jersey for the holidays, but Angela never got the chance to tell Mandy's father, Rick, that she'd be calling him Dad.

Two days before Christmas, on an unseasonably warm day, Rick and Tony took a ride on their motorcycles to pick up some spiced rum for the celebratory eggnog. Mandy opened the door to find Tony screeching into the driveway on his motorcycle. "Dad's gone down!" he screamed. "Call an ambulance!"

Mandy's mother, Lorri, grabbed the phone and thrust it into Mandy's hands. "You call 911!" she screamed. "It's what you do." Angela scrambled to find towels and bandages to take to the scene.

Following Tony, Lorri drove Mandy and Angela to the scene. Rick had failed to make a sharp curve on his motorcycle. He'd flown off his bike, crashing headfirst through a gazebo. The force of the impact knocked off his helmet. The scene was bloody, and it was clear to Angela, a trained EMT accustomed to dangerous accidents, that his injuries were devastating.

In the rural central New Jersey town, volunteer firefighters were maddeningly slow to arrive. They began to pull up one by one in their personal vehicles. Finally, a man with a radio in his car came on the scene and called for a medevac helicopter.

The EMTs arrived and cut Rick's clothes off. Lorri started yelling for someone to cover him up. "He's cold," she wailed. As Mandy held her mother back, they heard the beat of a helicopter. Two medics pulled a stretcher from the back of an ambulance.

"Why are they moving so slowly? Why aren't they doing CPR?" Angela wondered, agonized by the slow pace of the rescue. Overhead, the helicopter's engine began to grow faint. "They've called it off," she said flatly. "He's not going to make it." The EMTs slid the stretcher back in the ambulance. Rick had a severed brain stem, a perforated heart, and a bisected liver. He was dead.

Mandy begged Angela to tell her the details of what had happened. "I don't think I can . . ." Angela said. Then, "He's gone. There's nothing they can do." Angela watched the EMTs say to Mandy's mother the same words she had repeated to bereaved families so many times. "We've done everything we could." To Angela, it was so familiar but so inadequate. But there was nothing more anyone could say.

The focus of Christmas turned from presents and meals to funeral arrangements. On Christmas Eve, the family attended Midnight Mass at the Catholic church that Rick had attended. They took up an entire row. Mandy recalls these scenes from three years before with tears streaming from her brown eyes. "During the prayers and concerns, the priest mentioned my family. We all lost it. I was so sad, and I felt so bad being sad while everyone else was so happy because it was Christmas." Angela gently wipes a tear from Mandy's cheek and comforts her with a long embrace.

On Christmas Day, presents to and from Rick were under the tree. Mandy and Angela were stunned to learn what Rick had been doing the night before he died. He had stayed up late scraping the glitter off his stocking that spelled "Rick." In its place, he had written "Angela" in Elmer's glue and sprinkled it with silver glitter. He had run out of time to offer Angela this heartfelt gesture of acceptance while he was alive. And Angela had never told him that she was ready to call him Dad.

Three years later Mandy's family is slowly healing, and last Christmas her mother opened presents for the first time since Rick's death. Angela continues to see grizzly accidents with regularity—in her job in pediatric critical care transport services, in her training to become a paramedic, and in the National Guard treating wounded soldiers. But her personal connection to the dangers of a motorcycle accident makes the prospect of responding to that particular emergency especially daunting.

Mandy says she cries less than she used to when she thinks about her father's death and his belated acceptance of her marriage. She and Angela are building their lives in Kansas City, putting together a plan for the future. She is halfway through her master's degree in divinity. Mandy doesn't have the energy or the inclination to fight the Methodists to be ordained as a lesbian minister. Instead, she is thinking of becoming a deaconess. These laywomen have a long-standing, progressive tradition within the Methodist faith of working for civil rights and racial and gender equality, as well as in hospices and with AIDS patients. She's intrigued by an opportunity to go to Trinidad and work with the poor. "My god is guiding me somehow," says Mandy. "I'll know if it's time for me to move or to stay."

Angela's obligation to the National Guard will expire at about the same time that Mandy expects to finish divinity school. Angela hopes to have completed her training as a paramedic by then as well and thinks she may be ready to leave the Midwest—an idea that never appealed to her before.

Angela enjoys her military service. "I don't find much more gratifying work than what I do in the military," she explains. "There is something fun and rebellious about being in the military and being able to say, 'I'm a noncombatant, and I don't believe in this war.'

I made it clear that I was a conscientious objector, but that's not incompatible with what I do. I hear shell fire going off, mortar fire. And I get to take people away from it. I can say to people, 'I'm here to take care of you, and listen to your story, and tell you you're all right.' I don't have to feel bad about believing that."

But Angela won't be reenlisting. It has been a struggle having fewer rights than her heterosexual colleagues. When Angela is deployed, Mandy doesn't get the support that other spouses do. She's not entitled to family counseling, Angela doesn't get extra family pay, and Mandy can't shop on the base while Angela is gone.

Mandy and Angela are thinking of buying a house, so now they're facing some new questions. Can they get a loan from the Veterans Administration together? They're currently seeking a sympathetic lawyer who can help them explore these thorny legal questions discreetly. They take this trailblazing in stride. But then, Mandy and Angela have never shown an unwillingness to cover new ground together.

Richard and Perry

"We'll get chickens and then we'll get married."

On a bright, sunny day in March 2004, Richard Mullinax and Perry Pike walked up the stone steps of the Old Courthouse in Durham, North Carolina. With their lawyer leading the way and Richard's father following behind, the couple turned in to the county clerk's office and asked for a marriage license.

Two nervous clerks asked to see their driver's licenses, and the two men pulled out their wallets and laid them on the counter. "I'm terribly sorry," one clerk said, verifying on the licenses what they already knew: Richard and Perry were both men. "We will be unable to issue a marriage license according to North Carolina state law."

Their lawyer, Cheri Patrick, begged to differ. Richard and Perry, she said, met all the criteria listed on the application: They were unmarried, older than sixteen, not close kin, and mentally competent. The clerks summoned the registrar of deeds, and the registrar summoned the county attorney. Richard and Perry waited anxiously, shifting uncomfortably in the blazers and ties they so rarely wore. Thirty-six-year-old Richard wore his wavy brown hair gathered in a thick ponytail. His blazing blue eyes locked on Perry, his forty-one-year-old partner with wispy, dirty-blond hair and high, sculpted cheekbones. They waited while the clerks and registrar conferred in whispers. Finally, the county attorney turned and said, "Sure. You can give them an application."

For lack of a better place, Perry filled his name in the spot reserved for "Groom's Information," and Richard filled in the "Bride's." "I was shaking," says Richard. "It took forever. It was like I was trying to write with a pencil between my toes."

That March morning was the midpoint in Richard's and Perry's journey to be married. They had wrestled with whether two small-town country boys, both raised as God-fearing Southern Baptists, who had struggled to hide their attraction to men growing up, should become the public face of gay marriage in Durham. It's a quest that has elevated them to minor celebrity status among their activist and artsy friends, even though their completed application for a marriage license was quickly, though politely, denied.

Richard and Perry briefly pursued an appeal, arguing that although state law forbids same-sex marriage under North Carolina's "Defense of Marriage Act," nothing prohibits counties from

Perry and Richard

issuing marriage licenses. Prior to their march on the clerk's office, Richard and Perry had approached several gay and lesbian advocacy groups for support. "Everybody already knew we were a couple," says Perry. "We thought it was time to stand up against hate language." But national groups were directing their resources to states where they imagined greater success, and local groups discouraged them from moving forward and pushing their case too soon, fearing that it could lead to a backlash of more discriminatory laws. After just three months of legal wrangling, Richard and Perry didn't have the money to pursue their appeals.

They left the clerk's office that morning followed by a dozen friends who had gathered to support them. In addition to Richard's father, they included three elderly women who called themselves "The Church Ladies," a baby in a jester suit clutching a lemur puppet, and members of the local Parents and Friends of Gays and Lesbians Group. The county attorney was bemused by the scene, saying, "The next time y'all come down here, you should bring refreshments."

Richard laughed, and agreed. "We will," he said. "It'll be wedding cake."

They haven't been back to the clerk's office to slice the wedding cake yet, but Richard and Perry are still on a mission to spread the word about same-sex marriage. It is an essential step, they believe, in dispelling fear and discrimination against gay people. Both of their lives have been shaped by the reactions of family, friends, and clergy to their sexuality, and Richard and Perry are committed to making things easier for the generation of gay people growing up behind them. "The more we can continue to have the words *gay* and *lesbian* out there, the less stigma they have and the more we can change the culture of hate," says Perry. "But it's one step, one breath at a time."

Richard and Perry have gotten used to being squeaky wheels. Their entry into the Durham political scene began six years ago, when they lobbied the city for the opportunity to buy a dilapidated but historic two-family house that had been seized by the housing department. The Old North Durham Neighborhood was seeking more owner-occupied houses, and contrary to Richard's and Perry's fears, nobody seemed to bat an eye that they were two men looking to buy a house together. Nearby property owners joined forces with the couple to convince the city to forgive the property's back taxes, lower the price, and sell to Richard and Perry. It was a valuable civics lesson for the couple, showing them the power of community, and Richard and Perry have only gotten more involved in local politics since.

Richard is now housing chair of Old North Durham and co-chair of the neighborhood Partners Against Crime group. He has also become highly visible through his advocacy for—and creation of—public art. Two weeks before he and Perry sought their marriage license, he installed two female mannequins in wedding dresses under a flowered arch in Durham Central Park. Wrapped in silver lamé, the arch bore the words "Just Luv."

Perry and Richard were both active lobbyists in the effort to get both the city of Durham and Durham County to create domestic partner benefits for same-sex couples. "We saw how the process worked, and we saw how people changed their minds," says Richard. Those successes helped give them the courage to seek a marriage license, and they informed county commissioners of their intention. "The first time I mentioned it, one of the commissioners just looked at me and said, 'Oh, Richard. Don't do that.'"

That's the same reaction Richard got when he built a chicken coop in his backyard and began to challenge an ordinance prohibiting farm animals within the city limits. Richard doesn't want to keep noisy roosters, just hens that will lay fresh, organic eggs for the hearty skillet breakfasts he and Perry prepare together on weekends. Once again, he's using art to advocate for his position. With the blessing of a local ordinance he pushed for that allows for temporary public art installations, Richard erected a seven-foot-tall wire chicken sculpture in the park where his wire brides stood a year before. "We'll get chickens," says Richard, with confidence. "Then we'll get married."

Perry's real-life civics lessons came from his work with the Historic Preservation Society of Durham as educational facilitator. He helped create walking tours of the city's tobacco heritage, its role in the civil rights movement, and its rich arts and architecture scene. The experience brought Perry close to the city's movers and shakers and made him feel that his goal of changing laws was within reach.

Neither man is a Durham native. Perry found his way to this faded tobacco town from DeWitt, Arkansas, and Richard drove up from Winnsboro, South Carolina. They were set up in 1998 by mutual friends who gave each the other's phone number and urged them to call. Richard dialed first, one country accent phoning another. Their similar childhoods in rural southern towns were a point of immediate connection. So was their common experience growing up in conservative Southern Baptist churches.

After two weeks of phone conversations, Richard called Perry one evening while Perry was cooking dinner. "Why don't you come over?" Perry asked, and Richard did. It was a big step for Perry, who was still reeling from the end of a year-long relationship. And it was a welcome change for Richard, who hadn't been socializing much outside of his contact with coworkers at a Durham flower shop. Richard was a breath of fresh air for Perry. "My last boyfriend was totally about being put together," Perry recalls. "He was always well manicured; he even plucked his eyebrows. Then Richard walked in, wearing cutoff khakis with fringe hanging off them, a T-shirt with holes in it, and Indian sandals. He didn't look like he gave a shit about fashion. And I was like 'Yeah!' I was taken by his nonchalance."

Richard was taken by Perry's kindness and gentle manner—exactly what Richard had been drawn to in their phone conversations. After dinner, as they left Perry's apartment for a walk, Richard spotted a four-leaf clover and bent down to pick it up. He turned to offer it to Perry, who had found a four-leaf clover, too. To Richard, it was more than a sign of good fortune. "It was a sign of an ability we have in common," he says, an ability to find special things among the ordinary. "Perry was an old friend instantly."

Durham is a comfortable city for Richard and Perry, a progressive bastion in a conservative state, where they don't feel as if they have to hide their relationship. It's a far cry from the environments where they were both raised.

Perry grew up in rural Arkansas in the sixties and seventies. His attraction to men was something he thought he just had to get over. One summer, visiting his older sister in another small Arkansas town, he sought out the help of a minister at a charismatic Full Gospel church. The minister was a married man of thirty-six with two children. Perry was eighteen. He confessed to the minister that he was attracted to men. The minister responded by giving Perry a passionate kiss on the lips.

The kiss grew into a summer romance, one that Perry looks back on now with anger. "I have real issues with authority figures who abuse their power over others," he says. It was Perry's first sexual encounter with a man, and as far as Perry knows, it was the minister's too. Perry struggled at the summer's end with whether to go back to college. It required a tremendous exertion of his will to break free of the minister's emotional hold on him. But he did succeed in leaving and returned to Hendrix College. He heard nothing of the minister for another decade.

In 1992, Perry was living in Little Rock with his then partner. They befriended another couple, and at dinner one night, the conversation turned to a talk of the many southern towns they'd lived in. His friend David mentioned living in a town in Arkansas, the name of which Perry recognized as the minister's hometown. "Why did you move there?" he asked

"My partner was from that town, and he wanted to move back," David said

"What was his name?" asked Perry.

It was the same man who had taken advantage of the eighteen-year-old Perry. David and Perry put down their forks, and Perry felt the room begin to spin while David filled in the details of a four-year abusive relationship with the minister, who had left his wife by that time. It took years for David to leave him, and even as he failed to break free, one idea sustained him. One summer, when David was in high school, the minister had come to town with an eighteen-year-old blond boy who had sung a solo. When

David met the minister as an adult, he learned that the boy had been named Perry and that Perry was the minister's summer romance who had had the courage to pick up and leave. "I knew you'd left and gone back to college. I knew there was a gay person in the world who had made it," David told a stunned Perry. "For years, I told people I had a gay friend, and he had made it."

It still unnerves Perry to tell this story. The moral is clear to him. "We can question whether our life has meaning," he says, reaching up a long hand to push away the stray hair that has tumbled onto his forehead. "We come into contact with so many people in ways that are so glancing and so tangential. My being me was something David had drawn on for strength. It's important not to question whether we are ministering to others. We change people's lives."

Richard and Perry have been helping each other change. When they met, both men were burning out in stressful jobs they no longer found satisfying. Richard was working long hours and every holiday in a flower shop. Perry was growing weary of teaching.

"We took turns to jump from what we were doing," says Richard. Perry went first, after Richard recognized the toll the teaching profession was taking on him. "I told him, you're going to quit this. It's not good for you." Perry found the preservation society job and has continued to evolve professionally toward jobs that satisfy him spiritually. He pursued an internship at the University of North Carolina Hospitals as a chaplain and now he's seeking to become ordained as a minister in the Dances of Universal Peace. The dances are an interfaith worship experience, with each dance inspired by a different world religious practice, ranging from Cherokee to Catholic, Jewish to Pagan, Buddhist to Baptist. All the dances focus on peace, healing, and a celebration of life. "I'm not sure what door I want to open by being ordained this way," Perry says. But he does imagine performing weddings and perhaps pursing a hospice or prison ministry.

After Perry found his footing outside of teaching, he urged Richard to quit his unfulfilling job as well. Richard left the florist and began to pursue his vocation as what he calls a "yard artist." He builds stone walls and art installations around people's homes.

Their own yard is a gallery of Richard's work. The lot surrounding their historic Dutch Colonial home is a sea of found objects that Richard has transformed into art. Off the screen porch is an arrangement of hundreds of green glass bottles that form a circular labyrinth walkway. Behind that lies the empty chicken coop, crafted from pieces of previously used fence that Richard artfully cobbled together. A dirt cave Richard and Perry call the "hobbit hole" faces a pit that will become a koi pond. In the spring and summer, the grounds are carpeted with flowers: lilies, camellias, larkspur, viburnum, peonies, poppies, roses, flox, and columbine. Richard estimates there are more than two thousand daffodils in the yard. Vines reach up trellises Richard fashioned out of copper piping. Sufi prayer flags fly from another wooden trellis. On their wide, southern-style front porch are three bright orange Adirondack chairs of increasing size. Richard and Perry like to sit there with their mellow Akita dog, incongruously named Kitty, lazily stretched out between them.

It's a life Richard never could have imagined. He didn't know two men could build their lives together this way. And he certainly never imagined himself as a community activist, pushing for public art, city chickens, and same-sex marriage. "I was this quiet little church mouse," Richard says. Not just quiet but fearful. For many years he thought that because he was gay, his life would be bleak and he would die of AIDS. But in the midst of these fears, Richard met Perry, who was committed to celebrating his sexuality and his spirituality.

"Richard is really blossoming now," says Perry.

"Yes," agrees Richard. "But I'm a very late bloomer."

Now that he is in full bloom as a colorful and creative man, it's hard to imagine that Richard had a hint of shyness. At the 2004 Durham Christmas Parade, he was gliding down the street in full drag, marching with other members of his neighborhood group, spoofing the city's long association with the Bulls, a minor league baseball team. Along with a man wearing a sash proclaiming him to be a Basebull and others dressed as Adorabull, Istanbull, and Snowbull, Richard was Indomitabull, the long legs of this six-foot-two-inch man drawing envious catcalls from men and women alike. "I used to be afraid of people laughing at me and rejection," says Richard. "But once I realized it's only laughing, it doesn't matter if they're laughing at me or laughing with me."

Much of Richard's fear has stemmed from his family's rejection of him because he is gay. Even before he came out to them, he was plagued by the teachings of his conservative Southern Baptist family as he was growing up.

"I don't know how I didn't end up chanting their mantras," says Richard, marveling at the tolerance he has embraced in his own life.

Richard's choice of words makes Perry howl with laughter. "Honey, they wouldn't have even said 'chanting mantras'!"

Looking back over his childhood, Richard says that he knew when he was twelve that he was attracted to men. "I didn't know what to call it," he explains. "But I heard that it was bad." In high school, Richard ended friendships with other boys as soon as he found himself attracted to them. He tried dating several girlfriends, kissing them on occasion.

Richard moved out of his small town to attend Clemson University, where he began to come out in stages. He found himself drawn to the school's gospel choir and mustered the courage to join in his second year. Much to his surprise—and delight—he realized that nearly all the other men in the choir were gay. Richard found himself a new kind of minority in two ways. He was one of only a few white faces in the black choir, and he seemed to be the only man who hadn't acknowledged his homosexuality. "I started to think, 'Okay, you can be gay, but I won't be that way,'" recalls Richard, laughing at his own naïveté. Looking back, he thinks that the other, more experienced men in the choir must have looked at him as a little mouse for the cats to play with. Even though many were interested in him, he settled into a relationship with one man.

After Richard graduated with his degree in horticulture, he and his partner moved to Charlotte, North Carolina, and then to Durham. Publicly they were always just friends. Privately, they were lovers. When his partner announced he was moving back to South Carolina, Richard realized he had no interest in moving back and being closeted again.

Before graduation, Richard came out to his parents. He remembers his mother crying and crying, mourning her son's inevitable early death from AIDS. He told his father as his dad sat in his usual posture, reading the newspaper with the television blaring in the background. His father's response, Richard recalls, was "I hope you don't think I'm responsible for this."

"I told him, 'Man, if I still blamed you for everything, I wouldn't be able to speak to you. There's no blame.'" It was a pivotal moment, from which Richard and his father have nurtured a mutual acceptance and respect. But with his mother, who lives alone since his father moved out six years ago, the relationship has gone from strained to worse.

Perry is not welcome to stay in Richard's mother's house, so he rarely accompanies Richard down to South Carolina on family visits. Things are even worse next door to Richard's mother, at his sister Karen's house. "I'm not comfortable with homosexuality because it's a sin," she says. "It trivializes my own marriage relationship, because God has ordained marriage to be between a man and a woman."

What has been so hurtful for Richard is Karen's insistence that her children, fourteen and twelve, not spend much time with him—especially when he is with Perry. "I can't invite them down to stay in my house when I'm trying to teach my children this is wrong," says Karen, with sadness in her voice. "My brother is such a creative and wonderful person. I get distraught that my children don't get to spend much time with him." But Karen says that Richard's homosexuality has "crippled" the close relationship they had as children. "It's a wall we keep peeking above but can't get over," she says.

Even though Karen knows Richard wouldn't be happy in a relationship with a woman, she still thinks it would be the right thing for him to do. "It would be more natural, more biblical," she says. And some urges, she believes, people just have to resist. Karen is candid about her own moral battle with alcohol. "Even though alcohol is still something I want, I don't always pursue it," she says. "It's wrong to walk around drunk all the time."

As her children get older, Karen says they will be free to choose whether to pursue a relationship with their gay uncle. She knows her son and daughter love him and get very excited when they know Richard is coming to visit. But with every visit she's also firm with her children: "His behavior is wrong."

One of Richard's aunts went even further, e-mailing him that he and Perry were not welcome at a summer family reunion. She wrote,

How I hate to say this to you, but you and Perry would not be welcomed. You, yourself, would be, but not your lifestyle. Rick, I know that you want everyone to accept the way you are living, but we cannot (and I am not speaking just for myself. I have discussed this with others and have prayed about it) according to God's Word. That is our standard. I would write this to any of my kids if they were living the way you are. I would also write this to a heterosexual couple who were living together, unmarried and wanting to come. It's not what we want to bring into our family and so we would have to ask you not to come if you are planning on bringing Perry. . . . I'm sure that you do not understand our love for you. We pray for you all the time, that God's truth would be revealed to you so that you can understand and be set free from the lies you are believing. It hurts to have to say what I have said. But, before God, I cannot say otherwise.

Richard gets close to tears when he talks about his family and how his relationship with Perry has put this distance between them. "Being gay is about being made aware of my separateness continually," says Richard. But he's also somewhat forgiving and maintains hope that with a little more time, their acceptance will grow.

"It took me twelve years to admit to myself that I was gay," says Richard. From age twelve to twenty-four he was in denial about his own sexuality. "So I've told people in my family that they have twelve years to accept that I am gay." In the case of Richard's mother and sister, those twelve years have come to an end, and he believes that it is time for them to accept him for who he is.

The turmoil in Richard's family makes Perry grateful for the calm with which his parents have always accepted him. He came out to them his senior year in college with a clear message: If they degraded him, he'd never come back. His ultimatum wasn't necessary, Perry recalls, because "their love for me overrode any other objection."

In 1999, Perry's niece Janna invited him to stand with her in the place of a maid of honor during her riverboat wedding. Without hesitation, she asked Richard to come with Perry—and to make the wedding bouquet. "It was very moving to me," says Perry. "It said to me that she loves me for who I am."

Perry also contrasts the reaction from Richard's family with the efforts other people in their community have made to learn about same-sex loving relationships. Part of Perry's pastoral training program at UNC Hospital brings him into conversations with ministers from Baptist, evangelical, and Methodist churches. He says, "The evangelical minister, in particular, has reflected deeply on actually knowing a gay person, especially one who is a minister. He's been able to ask me questions he never had permission to even consider before. We've lunched on various occasions and he has a million inquiries, all heartfelt and genuinely curious. All the while both he and I know that I would not be invited to attend his church. And yet, I see that he's really struggling with his humanity versus his theology. I experience his love and concern for me as a person and his desire to make peace with who I am and what he believes. This is beautiful work to witness."

These types of conversations, though challenging, have become commonplace for Richard and Perry as they live a public life as a gay couple. "Sometimes, like with Richard's family conversation, there seems to be an impenetrable wall," says Perry. "Other times, like with my current professional conversation, transformation blooms. The secret and essential ingredient is the conversation. One conversation at a time, our hearts meet and the world changes through that alchemy."

Perry and Richard aren't interested in a religious wedding ceremony. They're both immersed in their own faiths, Richard in the

Methodist Church and Perry in the Dances of Universal Peace. What they're seeking are the legal status, protections, and privileges of a marriage recognized by the state. So to them it made sense to finally exchange the rings they'd once hoped to swap in Durham City Hall in San Francisco City Hall, the place they see as the Mecca of gay marriage.

In February 2004, a year after four thousand same-sex marriage licenses were granted at San Francisco City Hall, Richard and Perry went to the Bay Area on vacation. Without telling Perry, Richard had tucked their rings into his wallet before leaving North Carolina. He convinced Perry to visit the towering dome of City Hall. Standing on the steps, he pulled out their rings. The couple decided that that the steps weren't quite good enough as a location for their ceremony. Their old activist selves came to the fore, and Richard and Perry found their way into the office of Mayor Gavin Newsome, the brazen city leader who had declared gay marriage legal in his city the year before.

The mayor was out of town, but before long, Richard and Perry were joking with the people in the city clerk's office just as they had back in the Registrar of Deeds office in Durham. Richard laid on his irrepressible charm and told them the story of his and Perry's attempt to marry back home. The clerks watched as Richard and Perry swapped rings right outside the door to Gavin Newsome's office. They kissed, and left the mayor a note. It simply said,

Dear Mayor Newsome,

The weddings here gave us the courage to ask for one at home. That was not a possibility for us before you showed us it could be done.

Thank you,
Richard Mullinax and Perry Pike

Kate and Joanna

"My youngest is my lesbian."

As she ladles bowls of Irish stew at a Cape Cod St. Patrick's Day dinner, Anne Toran does not look like an activist. Her green knit dress declares that she is proud to be Irish. Her bright red shoes show her *joie de vivre*. But it is the plastic rainbow lei around her neck that hints there might be something more behind the sparkling blue eyes of this mother of six and grandmother of twelve.

On a March evening in 2004, just two months before same-sex marriage was to become a legal option for couples in Massachusetts, Anne was the hostess of Falmouth's Celtic Diversity Dinner, an event she helped found four years earlier out of frustration over gays being barred from marching in South Boston's famed St. Patrick's Day Parade. That rankled the sixty-seven-year-old advocate, who has also established a college scholarship for members of the Cape and Islands Gay and Straight Youth Alliance and spearheaded a movement to declare her Falmouth church a congregation that welcomes gay, lesbian, and transgender people.

It's quite an activist résumé for Anne, a retired school secretary who didn't turn political until she was in her fifties. Her transformation was spurred by her youngest child. "I have six daughters," boasts Anne, adding, "My youngest is my lesbian."

When Anne first learned that Kate was a lesbian sixteen years ago, she cried. "It wasn't because she was any less my baby. She is my baby," says Anne of her youngest daughter, now closing in on forty. "It was because I thought her life would be more difficult than my other daughters'. But it hasn't turned out that way."

Kate's coming out as a lesbian spurred Anne to come out as an activist. "My agenda from the day Katy told me she was a lesbian has been that this is one of my children, and she is the same as my other children, and she deserves the same of everything," says Anne. That has meant major changes for the lifelong Catholic, who attended parochial schools in the working-class suburbs of Boston where she grew up. She also shepherded each of her daughters through a Catholic upbringing in the summer resort town of Falmouth, where the Torans live year-round amid sandy beaches, lighthouses, ice-cream shops, and a quintessentially New England village green ringed by white-steepled churches and traditional Colonial and Victorian houses. "I knew nothing about homosexuality," she recalls.

Joanna, Saiyana and Kate

But as Anne explored more fully what it meant for her daughter to be a lesbian in our society, she began to turn away from the Catholic Church. "I began to question different things in the church," she recalls. "It wasn't there for me anymore as the mother of six daughters. I just wasn't happy with it."

At the same time, she was beginning to become active in the gay rights movement. She attended her first marches with Kate. She joined Parents, Families, and Friends of Lesbians and Gays (PFLAG), and she started writing letters to the editor. "The first letter I wrote was very scary to me," says Anne. "But now I just throw off letters to the editor as often as I can." At her first Gay Pride march, Anne met two people who opened her mind and her heart and inspired her to action. One was a rabbi; the other was a Unitarian Universalist minister from the Unitarian Universalist Fellowship of Falmouth. She has embraced that liberal religious philosophy ever since.

Anne was proudly in attendance when Kate, an urban planner living in Berkeley, California, and her partner, Joanna Totino, a science teacher, had a commitment ceremony at Anne's church in 1999. Four years later, Kate and Joanna had hoped to make their marriage legal in a summer visit to Massachusetts a few months after gay marriage became legal. They even had their blood tests and got a marriage license.

But Massachusetts governor Mitt Romney threw a monkey wrench into their plans. Romney argued aggressively that an antiquated Massachusetts law once used to prevent interracial couples from marrying prohibited Massachusetts officials from marrying out-of-state couples if their home states would not authorize their marriage.

With the legality of a marriage in question, Kate was hesitant to move forward. Back in California, Joanna was preparing to adopt their baby, Saiyana, to whom Kate had given birth the previous winter. They feared that any union that wasn't viewed as completely legal might put that adoption at risk. Part of Saiyana's name means "honorable," and they didn't want to do something that could be seen as dishonorable on her behalf. (Saiyana's name also means "eternal blossom." "It's a Berkeley name," Kate explains, laughing. "We combined a couple of names and meanings that we liked. It has a lot of depth and it sounds nice.")

Kate and Joanna had missed the brief window of opportunity when marriages were being performed across the bay in San Francisco. Saiyana had been born just eight weeks before, and they were preparing for a two-week yoga retreat in Belize. But even without legal marriage rights, Kate and Joanna's commitment to each other is clear. And Anne has never questioned that their union is every bit as sacred and valid as those of her older daughters. On December 20, 2003, the day Kate gave birth to Saiyana, Anne's oldest daughter, Tina, got married in Falmouth. "What a day!" Anne says, sighing with exhaustion at the memory. "I was wiped out!"

Anne's husband, Fred, toasted his two daughters at the wedding. He called his oldest and his youngest "my alpha and my omega."

Anne doesn't reflect on her daughter being a lesbian with any hand-wringing or regret. To the contrary, she describes Kate's orientation as a wonderful opportunity for the whole family. "It has been a growing experience for me," says Anne. "It has been powerful and awesome."

Those two words describe Anne herself. Though petite and trim, Anne conveys muscle and intensity that she never knew she could. "I was this mousy little thing that had no voice, and now I never shut up," she admits, chuckling. Her pen was working overtime in the months leading up to the Massachusetts Supreme Court decision that legalized same-sex marriage, drafting letters to her state representatives and local papers in support of gay marriage.

Her gallant husband, a silver-haired, gracious gentlemen in his mid-seventies, supports their lesbian daughter and her marriage implicitly. But he doesn't share Anne's passion or energy for activism. Fred has maintained membership in the Catholic Church, attending Saturday masses so he can accompany his wife to her activist church on Sundays. "They sing too many verses," he says and winks, poking good-natured fun at the earnest folks in his wife's Unitarian Universalist church. But ever the host, he was a central player in Anne's Diversity Dinner. He escorted the 120-plus guests to their tables and ensured that they had plenty of stew. He joined in proudly during the Irish sing-a-long, crooning "Too-ra-loo-ra-loo-ra!" and "Gypsy Rover." He teared up with the rest of the crowd as a guitarist sang a lullaby by the Unitarian Universalist minister Fred Small:

You can be anybody you want to be
You can love whomever you will
You can travel any country where your heart leads
And know I will love you still
You can live by yourself, you can gather friends around
You can choose one special one
And the only measure of your words and your deeds
Will be the love you leave behind when you're done.

By the end of the night, the stewpots were empty. Sleeping children were slung over their parents' shoulders. And Anne's dinner had raised $729 for the Cape Cod Free Clinic and the AIDS Support Group of Cape Cod.

Before creating the tradition of the Diversity Dinner, Anne spearheaded a three-year movement within her church to make her fellowship a "welcoming congregation," one that accepts heterosexual, gay, lesbian, bisexual, and transgender people. "We're a church of open minds," says Anne, "but we still had to turn some people's ideas around." Together with a lesbian couple from her church, Anne set up meetings to talk to other church members about their experience as a gay couple and their fears for the future.

Once the church voted officially to become welcoming, Anne decided they should go even further. She established the Diversity Dinner and then created a Solidarity Sunday to coincide with National Coming Out Day in October. The message is simple: "Somebody you care about is gay. Please be supportive of them." She has also endorsed changes in the religious education curriculum that help even the smallest children learn about diverse families. "The children make a rainbow banner, and we wrap the entire church in it," says Anne.

Having worked in schools for twenty-eight years, Anne's heart is never far from education. She helped establish a Gay Straight

Alliance Scholarship for students on Cape Cod and its nearby islands. In 2004, the scholarship amount reached $2,000. "The kids are really learning," says Anne. "Being gay is not going to be a big deal in another generation."

Through all her events, letters, and committees, Anne has touched many lives and done significant person-to-person work for marriage equality. But certainly the life she has touched the most has been her daughter's. "Katy is the most proud of all. It validates her," says Anne. "All of this makes my heart sing. My youngest daughter is a joy in my life, and I'm so happy for her that she is in a wonderful, loving relationship."

Kate and Joanna own a renovated bungalow in Berkeley, a mile from the wooded campus of the University of California. Saiyana, blowing bubbles with a plastic toy, toddles in their fenced backyard through the pagoda and the gazebo dripping with jasmine flowers and wisteria.

Kate is the only one of her five sisters to leave Cape Cod. The rest still live in the same zip code as her parents. At times she misses the closeness of the family she was raised in. But her sisters and her parents are frequent visitors. Some of her sisters flew out to help Joanna and Kate move, and one brother-in-law came out to lay new ceramic tile in their remodeled, spacious kitchen. And there are the annual summer visits to the Cape, when the whole family converges to mark Katy's and Joanna's return.

The Torans have embraced Joanna like one of their own, even jokingly calling her the "seventh sister." The acceptance couldn't be more opposite from what Joanna has experienced in her own family. Joanna's parents, Italian immigrants who still live in her Massachusetts hometown, wouldn't attend her commitment ceremony. They didn't even respond to the invitation she mailed them. And they don't recognize Saiyana as their granddaughter.

"It's sad for me, but I've come to accept it," says Joanna, who is forty-five. She has olive skin that has been bronzed by the California sun and her deep brown eyes sadden when she talks about her family, even as she says that she has made peace with their condemnation of her life and her loved ones. Joanna makes a point each year during their annual trip to Cape Cod to visit her parents for a day in southeastern Massachusetts. "I could disassociate from my family completely. But I feel compassion for them. They're losing a close relationship with me and Kate and Saiyana and Ariel."

Their older daughter Ariel was born when Joanna was twenty-two. Joanna had a brief relationship with Ariel's father that ended when they both started seeing other women. Ariel, who now works with the deaf at Gallaudet University, was raised in the lesbian community, flying back each year to visit her father in Massachusetts. Kate and Joanna still marvel at the accepting community that nurtured her. Conversations with her friends at a camp for children of gay and lesbian people often centered on topics such as whose grandparents accepted them and whose didn't and who among them knew their donors. Chants on the camp bus were also different than those popular in other camps. One summer, girls jokingly yelled out the bus window to passing cars asking, "Are you my donor?"

"They had such an awareness of who their families are and such open discussions about them," says Kate. Joanna and Kate are trying to foster a similar openness in little Saiyana. Her donor is a neighborhood friend, whom Saiyana lovingly calls "Papi." He and his partner care for her once a week at their Berkeley home, where she loves to help them with the goats, chickens, and ducks they raise in their backyard. Papi is a central part of a tight network of friends who make up Saiyana's family. Joanna and Kate have a written agreement with Saiyana's biological father that Kate is the parent. "He signed over paternity rights, so he's not the father in the legal sense," says Joanna. "The legal boundaries are clear, so we don't feel any risk in he and Saiyana having a relationship. He's a person of such integrity; we want them to spend time together."

Joanna continues, "We have a vision of not being so nuclear. We want other adults to take responsibility in being a part of Saiyana's life." They call it a Bay Area Family, a network of adults—gay and straight, related and unrelated—who have created close familial connections with one another. Similar families are increasingly springing up in the San Francisco area. "There's an expanding idea of what it means to be a family," says Joanna. She and Kate each work a four-day week so they can spend a weekday with their daughter, and Saiyana attends a day-care center three days a week. When she visits Massachusetts in the summers with her mothers, Saiyana has her Cape Cod Bay Area family too. She is surrounded by aunts, uncles, cousins, and of course, her doting grandparents, Anne and Fred. Ariel was always embraced with that loving acceptance from Kate's family as well.

Kate shares her mother's wide, warm smile. From across the country, Kate has beamed with an almost maternal pride as she has watched her mother grow. "She had a whole transformation after I was in college," says Kate. "My sisters and I joke about it—that I'm the favorite because I'm the lesbian daughter!

"She needed to find her own voice," Kate says, recalling the strain her mother suffered living in the shadow of her father, Fred—the Republican, the public figure, the teacher, the coach. "At some point, my mother really needed to find her own voice and her own values. She started exploring feminism and politics." Anne enrolled in a program at Cape Cod Community College for women in transition and blossomed. "She got really politically active around gay issues and peace and freedom. The gay issues are really close to her heart."

Even before Anne's rebirth as an activist, Kate always remembers her mother being loving and accepting of her, even though she wasn't the same dress-wearing sort of girl as her five older sisters. "I was a little tomboy, and she always let me be that." When Kate came home from school complaining that she couldn't go upside down on the jungle gym in skirts, her mother let her wear pants—even though the other girls never had gone to school dressed like that. "I'm the youngest, and I was a little bit spoiled," Kate says, smiling at the memory.

Many adult children might bristle at a parent taking on their cause so completely. But Kate and Anne have never competed with each other in activism. Kate is proud of her mother and the way she has shown her support. It is an extension of the unconditional love Anne has always given her.

But having a straight mother who is more strident than her lesbian daughter does have its comical moments. Anne gets Kate involved in events that she would never participate in on her own. Kate laughs about a fund-raiser in Provincetown where her mother was Kate's entrée in to the world of Cape Cod's beautiful queer people. "She was dragging me around this deck party introducing *me* to everyone! She even introduced me to Kate Clinton!" Kate was delighted to meet the well-known lesbian comedian.

What impresses Kate, however, is not the people her mother knows but what her mother does. At that deck party, her mother was talking about the scholarship fund and the welcoming congregation and working with gay and lesbian kids. "She's not a holier-than-thou type of person," says Kate. "She's so warm and loving, everyone is happy to be around her."

It's the kind of mother Kate and Joanna want to be to Saiyana and Ariel. "Unconditional love is something my mother is so good at providing," says Kate. "That is something we want to reproduce."

Tom and Phuoc

"I don't want to be a second-class citizen."

Tom Duke left Vietnam in 1970 to the roar of jet engines in a Boeing 707 commercial jetliner. His two-year tour of duty in Vietnam with Naval Intelligence had come to an end, and he was headed back home to Portland, Oregon, and a final six months of duty at the National Security Agency.

Phuoc Lam left Vietnam in 1987 in silence, huddled in a rickety wooden boat with forty other refugees under cover of darkness. He didn't know where the seas would take him. What mattered was what he was leaving behind: Saigon, the aftermath of war, a government that had held his father in jail for eight years.

It's hard to say exactly what brought Tom and Phuoc (pronounced "Fook") together, separated as they were by age, culture, distance, and history. They see it as fate, or karma, or maybe plain old luck. Phuoc was the first of this unlikely couple to return to Vietnam, searching out family and looking for the familiar in a country where nothing seemed the same. Among the countless changes Phuoc encountered—more cars and pollution and a greater disparity between the rich and the poor—computers had arrived. From Hanoi, he checked his e-mail to find a message from Tom that had flown from Tom's home computer on Washington's rainy Olympic Peninsula to an Internet café in steamy Hanoi. It read, "Phuoc, would you marry me?"

Since they had started living together five years before, Tom and Phuoc had never been so far apart. Phuoc was taking a risky trip back to the country he had fled as a teenager. Back home, Tom was lonely and worried. He couldn't stop imagining that Phuoc would be facing the same wartime horrors that he had seen himself thirty-five years ago. For the first time, Tom felt an enormous void in their relationship. He wanted to be lawfully bound to Phuoc; he wanted to be married.

It was March 2004, and while Phuoc was half a world away, Tom was reading about same-sex couples preparing to marry in Massachusetts and having weddings in San Francisco, Portland, Oregon, and New Paltz, New York. "I started freaking out that we had no legal protections," says Tom. His pale blue eyes behind wireless glasses rest on Phuoc, a slender, youthful thirty-two-year-old with tousled black hair and funky rectangular glasses. At first Tom had imagined that when Phuoc returned they would make pilgrimages to all the places where gay weddings were being per-

Phouc and Tom

formed and get married in each of them. But then Tom realized that what he really wanted was to get married at home.

From Hanoi, Phuoc e-mailed back his response: "Marry? Yes!" They were still separated by an ocean for several weeks to come, and while Phuoc toured Vietnam, reconnecting with family he hadn't seen in two decades, Tom grew restless at home and was inspired to action. He contacted the American Civil Liberties Union to see how he could join the cause. He pictured himself stuffing envelopes, maybe making a few phone calls promoting gay and lesbian civil rights. Instead, he was asked to join a lawsuit pushing for equal marriage in the Evergreen State.

Wishing for rights is one thing; actively fighting for them is another. Tom and Phuoc weighed whether to put their names on the cause they so passionately believed in. Neither had ever been a public crusader, and both were more prone to private reflection and pursuits. At fifty-seven, Tom had been a psychotherapist for twenty-four years, working quietly and discreetly on other people's issues. And to complicate matters, Phuoc's large, close-knit Vietnamese family seemed not to be aware that he was gay. Phuoc is also acutely aware of his minority status and regularly feels the sting of subtle discrimination as the only Vietnamese person in a small rural town. But ultimately, the couple's concern for justice trumped their need for total anonymity, and they joined the lawsuit, *Castle v. State*, soon after Phuoc's return from Vietnam.

Tom and Phuoc met online in an Internet chat room. Tom had only had a computer for two weeks before he wandered into a virtual discussion among Asian gay men. Amid the English chatter, Tom typed a message to Phuoc in Vietnamese. A connection was made, and a spark soon followed. Tom and Phuoc exchanged e-mail addresses and started to write directly, once a day at first, but soon they were writing two or three times a day. "If I didn't hear from him, I'd start to freak out," recalls Tom.

Phuoc was living a solitary existence in Valdosta, Georgia. A recent graduate of the Hilton College of Hotel and Restaurant Management at the University of Houston, Phuoc had been recruited to work as a civilian food service manager at U.S. Army bases. "I was the only Asian I could see for miles around," he recalls. For him, the chat room was a way to reach out to people he knew he'd never meet on the base.

For Tom, the appeal of the chat room came from his memories of the Asian families and culture that he had seen in Vietnam. "I was impressed by Asian family values," he says. "Plus I knew Asian people have a lot of respect for older people." Though Tom was then in his early fifties, Phuoc didn't learn that for some time. And even though Phuoc had gone to the chat room seeking an Asian connection, he was glad to come out of it with Tom's e-mail address. Their daily messages distracted Phuoc from the isolation that tormented him in Georgia.

They decided to exchange photographs, even though Tom feared this would end their connection. Tom was startled by Phuoc's good looks: thick, short black hair, cut bluntly over a slender face with a gentle smile. "I thought, Oh my God! He's so cute!" remembers Tom. Phuoc was intrigued by Tom's photo as well. Tom has close-cropped white hair, a trim beard and mustache, and a gaze that's at once intense and gentle. "I'm a very visual person, but I knew the picture wouldn't tell me the whole story," says Phuoc. "I wanted to see him in person."

They began to talk on the phone—stiff, awkward conversations that were nothing like the easy e-mail exchanges that had become their routine. The conversations slowly grew more comfortable, even when Phuoc was in tears about how much he disliked his life in Valdosta. Six months after their chat-room introduction, they decided it was time to meet.

Tom flew to Jacksonville, Florida, nervous as a cat. By now, he felt devoted to Phuoc and became anxious when he wasn't at the airport to greet him. But Phuoc was there, hiding behind a chair to observe Tom from afar before introducing himself. "I knew it was Tom. He was the only person in the airport in Birkenstocks," Phuoc says, laughing. "He had to be from Seattle."

Their first weekend was in a beach hotel, nervously getting to know each other face-to-face. The awkwardness disappeared on Jekyll Island, Georgia, where they camped. They found they could effortlessly pitch a tent together and cook an outdoor meal. Tom saw the first fireflies in his life. Phuoc started to imagine a life outside of Valdosta.

Trips across the country became routine for Phuoc and Tom. On Tom's second trip to Jekyll Island, they exchanged rings on the beach. When Phuoc summoned the courage to leave his unhappy job in Georgia, he headed home to Houston, to Tom's surprise. "I was so worried I'd lose him. Asian families have such gravity," says Tom, recalling that that familial closeness is part of what drew him to an Asian partner in the first place. "I thought that if he went back home, he'd never get out."

A few months later, with all his things in storage, Phuoc did get out. To give himself plenty of time to mull over his decision to move to the Northwest, Phuoc traveled by train with a one-way ticket from Houston to Seattle.

Phuoc is used to slow, meandering journeys. That is how he made his way to the United States in the first place.

At age fourteen, Phuoc was nearing the age when Vietnamese boys were drafted. It was a frightening prospect for his dissident family. His mother, an English teacher, had supported her four children while their father, an aerospace engineer, served eight years in a harsh Vietnamese prison for sedition. One by one, Phuoc's mother was turning her children over to strangers in an act of faith that they would be able to lead a better life somewhere else. Anywhere else.

Phuoc was the third to go, six years after his brother and one year after his older sister. His mother awoke him one night, bid him good-bye, and watched him leave their Saigon house with two men who led Phuoc to a single-hulled wooden boat. Just thirty feet long, the rickety craft would soon hold forty people hunched together beneath a camouflaged tarp as they made their way down the Mekong Delta and into the South China Sea.

"These boats aren't meant to hold so many bodies, and they don't have enough gas to get to an island," says Phuoc. "They will only hold up for three or four days." The passengers hoped for enough time to reach international waters and be rescued. A commercial freighter spotted the boat, which had begun to sink after four days at sea. Crew members helped the refugees onboard and transported them to an oil platform, where they spent a night before another boat came and took Phuoc and his stranded countrymen to a refugee camp in Pulao Bidong, Malaysia.

A special aura seems to hover over Phuoc, protecting him and guiding him and his family. The good fortune that led to his boat's rescue led to a UNICEF relief worker, who inquired whether he was related to a girl with the same surname who had passed through the camp months before. It was his sister, and she had already advanced to the next stop for Vietnamese refugees, Kuala Lumpur. Within two months, brother and sister were reunited, living together in the same hut and waiting to learn where their home would be. They took classes together at "Quarantine U," the nickname for the camp where the refugees were registered, got medical checks, and took classes in Western culture, learning about everything from schools to hot-water taps.

The year that Phuoc was born, 1972, his uncle had left Vietnam on an education visa and never returned. He had settled in Houston, so that is where Phuoc's older brother was resettled and where Phuoc and his sister were heading. Another long journey began as the siblings boarded a plane bound for Hong Kong, then for San Francisco, and finally for Houston, where the uncle, aunt, and cousins they had never known met them at the gate.

Within a year, Phuoc's parents and younger sister left Saigon in boats as well. In all, twenty members of Phuoc's family escaped from Vietnam. They all survived.

Tom knew he would be drafted to serve in Vietnam, so he enlisted in the Navy. He had flunked out of the University of Oregon, unable to manage the rigors of paying his own way, so his deferment was up. "Today if this had happened, I wouldn't have been drafted, because I would have been out as a gay man," says Tom. "But there was no culture to support gay people. I had feelings, but I didn't know how to act on them. I thought I was just like everyone else."

In the Navy, Tom was sent to the Defense Language Institute in Monterey, California, where he studied the Vietnamese language, and to the National Security Agency in Washington, D.C. He was trained in naval intelligence and as a noncombatant with a top-secret clearance to work on breaking codes. Tom looks back on his time there as "an interesting experience" and a welcome break from the difficulties of growing up with an alcoholic father. "I grew up in such a crazy scene in my family, being in Vietnam was much more predictable."

"I found ways to stay sane over there," he says. He made close friends and he learned to surf at China Beach. He never had a gay relationship in Vietnam. He worried that if he did and were found out, he would be sent to the front lines.

After his tour was up, Tom headed back to Portland, Oregon, and it was as if none of his war experiences had ever happened. He started college again and moved in with his girlfriend. He earned a bachelor's degree and then a master's degree in clinical psychology from Antioch University. At the same time, his eyes started opening to the burgeoning gay movement that was growing up alongside feminism and antiwar protests. He began to have relationships with men.

Tom came out to his family in his late twenties. His father had died when he was a teenager and his mother has been dead for twenty years. His mother appeared accepting of his sexual orientation, as was his sister. But he and his sister are not close. "I feel like Phuoc's family is my family," says Tom. They have embraced Tom. None of them has ever mentioned the word *gay*.

"In Vietnamese culture, homosexuality is worse than AIDS. It is the worst disease you can contract," says Phuoc. "There is a lot of homophobia." He noted the irony of this when he visited Saigon as an adult. In the evenings, gay culture pervades the city and provides music, restaurants, and clubs for straight people to enjoy. But even straight people who frequent the clubs do not talk about homosexuality, Phuoc says, except to condemn it.

Phuoc knows who his gay family members are. His father has ten siblings, and Phuoc knows that four of them have gay sons. "There is no need to discuss it," says Phuoc. "We're all happy. We're all loving."

Tom has worked as a clinical psychologist with his own private practice since 1988, and he talks freely and openly about his own feelings. He was angry at first about Phuoc's unwillingness to be direct with his family about the nature of their relationship. He wanted their love for each other to be known, and he wanted to be able to sleep in the same bedroom as Phuoc when they made family visits. But over time, Tom has come to understand the value that Phuoc's family, like many Vietnamese families, places on subtlety. "Not everything needs to be spoken," says Tom. He has been embraced by Phuoc's family, welcomed into their home on many occasions, and Tom and Phuoc host Phuoc's parents on their visits to the Northwest. Tom has come to understand that even though Phuoc has not told his parents about their relationship, it doesn't mean he loves Tom any less. And he respects Phuoc's concern that if he tells his parents he will add to the burdens they already carry, having endured the Vietnam War and the fall of Saigon.

Public perception worries Tom too. This fear centers not on their same-sex relationship but on their twenty-six-year age difference. "I didn't want people to think I was a child molester," says Tom. "And I didn't want anyone to think I was his sugar daddy." Phuoc especially bristles at that idea; he prides himself on being driven, hardworking, and self-sufficient. His current venture is a sporting goods store that he and Tom bought and Phuoc manages with a close eye and an entrepreneurial flair. It's a business Phuoc would like to focus on environmentally friendly and sweatshop-free products. "All my cousins back home are sweating for the shirt that I am wearing," says Phuoc, some of his English words tinged with a Vietnamese accent and others with a Houston twang. "I want to have a bigger impact on society and sustainable living."

After initially being reluctant to join the Freedom to Marry lawsuit against the State of Washington, Phuoc now wants to make an impact on society by helping to create equal marriage rights for same-sex couples. "I don't want to be a second-class citizen," he says.

March 9, 2005, was a historic day for Tom and Phuoc. On this clear, blue-skied day, they put on suits and ties and, along with the eleven other plaintiff couples, gathered at the Washington Supreme Court in Olympia. Outside the courthouse, a crowd of five thousand protesters swarmed. Members of the Washington Christian Coalition rallied opponents of same-sex marriage, holding signs saying that marriage was for "One Man, One Woman," and leading prayers and hymns.

Phuoc was angry, frustrated, and nervous. Lawyers for the ACLU, arguing in favor of same-sex marriage, gathered with the plaintiffs. To navigate the crush of protesters and supporters and get into the crowded courtroom, the plaintiffs and the lawyers joined hands and snaked through the crowd. As frightening as the protests were, Phuoc and Tom found the supporters inspiring. "These were people I didn't know supported me," says Phuoc, smiling at the thought of the strangers in rainbow T-shirts and pink triangles who cheered them on.

In the lawsuit, *Castle v. State*, the State of Washington is appealing a September 2004 ruling by a superior court judge that says that legal barriers to marriage for same-sex couples violate the state constitution's guarantee of equal treatment for all citizens. In his lower court ruling, Judge Richard Hicks rebuffed arguments that same-sex marriage destabilizes the family, noting that same-sex couples have already been found to serve as capable foster and adoptive parents. He argued that granting marriage equality to same-sex couples strengthens the community, writing, "Our fundamental principle is that we share the freedom to live with and respect each other and share the same privileges or immunities. We need each other."

In the crowded courtroom, Tom and Phuoc were riveted by the ACLU lawyers' oral arguments and the judges' questions. Tom imagined a day when Phuoc would be entitled to Social Security survivorship benefits if he died. Phuoc reflected on how he has grown resentful of paying his income taxes because he can't enjoy the same civil rights as other citizens.

When the arguments were over, Tom and Phuoc made their way once again past the throng of protesters, a little less daunted now that they had the words of the ACLU lawyers ringing in their ears. By the end of the session in the courtroom, Phuoc's anger toward the protesters had dissipated. "They were just doing their homework for their religion," Phuoc said. "That's the nature of fundamentalism."

Tom and Phuoc returned home to face at least a six-month wait for the court's decision. Their Olympic Peninsula home is a simple, white rectangular building that Tom built himself on a remote six-acre meadow. At the edge of their deck is a hot tub that affords stunning views of verdant countryside, framed by Douglas fir trees and dotted with the yellow flowers of wild mustard plants. Hummingbirds flutter by and blue herons feed in their pond. The yard is framed with daffodils and their vegetable garden is nearly ready for the planting of another summer's crop.

Tom and Phuoc are thinking of leaving this idyllic setting. Their dream is to sell off the house and buy a recreational vehicle to travel the country. They would like to spend more time in Houston with Phuoc's family and return to Jekyll Island, where they exchanged rings when they first fell in love. They know their wanderlust won't last forever, so they plan to retain most of the land and return someday to build another simple home in which to grow old, when they hope to be legally married.

Tom and Phuoc haven't sorted out the irony or coincidence or karma that brought them together: an American Vietnam War vet with a Vietnamese boat person. Phuoc's Buddhism advises him that fate has united them. Then he jokingly adds that maybe being married to a soldier whose army laid waste to his country is punishment for something he did in a past life.

Tom sometimes sees his devotion to Phuoc as an act of atonement for what the United States did to Vietnam. "But I couldn't ever make up for what we did to them," he says. His voice trails off, his pale blue eyes gazing across the Strait of Juan de Fuca to an island where the U.S. military stores artillery waiting to be loaded on to ships bound for Iraq. Whether there is a cosmic significance to their relationship, its present meaning is clear. It's about love. In Vietnamese, *vé nhà* means "return home." In Vietnam, you don't *go* home, you *return* there. When Phuoc left Saigon after his month-long visit in 2004, it didn't feel like his home anymore. It didn't even officially have the same name—Saigon had been renamed Ho Chi Minh City. But Phuoc did finally know where home was. He was going back to Washington. Back to Tom. He was returning home. *Vé nhà.*

Beth and Genesis

*"I knew I would be able to be gay
the day I was financially independent."*

The cameras are rolling under the desert sun. On a purple yoga mat, Beth Shaw breathes deeply, gracefully stepping into the moon pose, feet apart, arms raised to the wide, cloudless sky. "Inhale and exhale," she tells the camera. "Bring your breath together with movement. Bring the body and the mind together."

The camera pulls back from Beth to show a fit man and woman behind her, imitating her every move. In the background is a sparkling pool, a stone Buddha, seven palm trees, and the San Jacinto Mountains rising abruptly over Palm Springs, California.

Beth, thirty-eight, is recording her company's latest yoga video, *YogaFit's Flex and Flow*. Watching through the sliding-glass doors of their ranch-style weekend home is Beth's wife, twenty-eight-year-old Genesis Moss. In black yoga pants and a peach tank top, she's instructing a photographer on the design of the video case and cooling down from a video shoot of her own.

In this same backyard in October 2004, Beth and Genesis were married to each other on a perfect, starlit evening. They were 120 miles east of their weekday home in Hermosa Beach, where Genesis wilts from the bustle and demands of Los Angeles life and Beth tires of the energy it takes to live in the straight world. The

Palm Springs house was the ideal place for Beth and Genesis to wed. It's right in the middle of this resort city, which attracts a mix of gay and golf vacationers, and it's a welcome haven where two glamorous lesbians can get away from the stress of big-city heterosexual life.

"In L.A., if we go to a restaurant together, guys hit on us and want to buy us drinks," says Genesis, shaking her head and sending her blond ponytail swinging. "Here we can walk down the street holding hands, and nobody stares."

Beth and Genesis are both used to being stared at. For eleven years, Beth, a tall, muscular woman with long, highlighted brown hair, has been a high-profile, yoga fitness trainer. Her company, YogaFit, has a studio and a line of videos, accessories, books, and apparel. She travels internationally, training instructors and promoting her brand of yoga, which combines Eastern stretching, poses, and breathing with strength training and aerobics.

Genesis rode the first wave of reality television, appearing on MTV's *The Real World* in 1997. In most of its fifteen seasons, *The*

Genesis and Beth

Real World has reserved one of its seven slots for a gay man or lesbian on the show, which unites a cast of under-twenty-four-year-olds for three months of round-the-clock filming. On her application for the show, Genesis was clear with the producers that she was a lesbian. But something about her appearance, her cheerleader background, and her sexual identity didn't add up for the show's producers. "They typecast me as the attractive lesbian who would turn straight on the show," says Genesis, rolling her round, turquoise eyes. It's an expectation she continues to encounter and which makes the climate in Palm Springs all the more attractive. "Straight guys think they can turn me straight," she says. "Especially when they find out I've never been with a guy, they view me as a trophy."

Almost everything about Palm Springs is luxurious. On the edge of the dry Mojave Desert, its lushly watered lawns are carpeted with green grass and ringed with palm trees and fragrant flowers. Palm Canyon Drive is lined with coffee shops and art galleries. The surrounding sand seems to absorb all sound, leaving a tranquil and sunny silence in the day and a quiet starry dome at night. But the biggest luxury for Beth and Genesis is the freedom to be anonymous and themselves. "When we're here, we can surround ourselves with people who support our relationship," says Beth, a self-described workaholic. Many of her sentences are punctuated with the ring of her cell phone, calls from her lucrative Los Angeles–based business, which whirs away even in her absence. It's a business that encourages people, through yoga and exercise, to let go of their expectations, competitiveness, and judgment. With the same words, she describes her philosophy of exercise as well as the tenets of life she and Genesis strive to weave into their marriage.

Beth and Genesis spend a lot of time in sunny places. The met in 2001 in Orlando, Florida, at a birthday party of a mutual friend. Genesis was there with her first wife, a successful hairstylist and salon owner named Paige, who was sixteen years older than Genesis. Beth and Genesis had an instant attraction to each other, and they began to flirt, without regard for who was watching. Genesis and Beth had swapped e-mail addresses and immediately began to correspond on Beth's return to California. But Genesis found the out-of-wedlock attraction as troubling as Paige did. She put an end to the e-mails and decided to pursue couple's counseling with Paige. She wanted to devote her energies to saving her marriage.

Paige, however, didn't share the same determination. Almost a year later, Genesis left Orlando for a month to film another reality television show, *Battle of the Sexes*. When she returned, Paige had fallen in love with her best friend, an attorney named Lynn, and Genesis had nowhere to go. She'd lost her job as a graphic designer and now her relationship. She thought of Beth and e-mailed her for the first time in a year. Within a week, Beth flew back to Florida. A week after Beth went home, Genesis flew to Los Angeles. "Then Beth told me she didn't do long-distance relationships," Genesis recalls. "She'd done that with a woman in San Francisco and it didn't work." So three weeks after her e-mail to Beth, Genesis moved in with her in Southern California.

Both women were surprised at the speed of their relationship, and they decided to proceed with caution and start the relationship with couples counseling rather than wait for it to end that way. "We were having sex day and night, but we didn't really know each other," says Genesis. "The counseling helped us learn to communicate. We were already in love, and we wanted to make it work." Two years later, they were planning a wedding.

Their ceremony was a simple affair. Sixty friends gathered in the backyard of their Palm Springs home. The evening was illuminated by the pool lights and by tiki torches scattered about the lawn. Both brides wore white. Genesis was striking in a shimmering full-length gown with an open back, and Beth glowed in a three-quarter-length sheath with spaghetti straps and a layered, ruffled hemline. They vowed to make each other happy for as long as they could. Their justice of the peace was Lynn, the woman Genesis's first wife had left her for. Paige and Lynn had flown out from Orlando to bless the union. Despite the turbulence of the past, the four of them have grown to be as close as family.

Beside the pool, Beth and Genesis had created a Buddhist-style altar, using the same statue that later provided a backdrop for the yoga video. Beth and Genesis lit candles to symbolize fire, lit incense to represent air, and laid their bouquets beneath the statue as a gift in exchange for Buddha's blessing of their union. Their two tiny dogs were ring bearers. Numi, a Boston terrier, and Ping, a Chinese pug, both sported miniature tuxedos, to which Beth and Genesis tied their rings.

Their dogs were there, their friends were there, but very little family was there. Beth's mother, who works for YogaFit, was in attendance. But Genesis hadn't invited any of her family. She knew there was no point.

Genesis was raised by her grandparents in Gulfport, Mississippi. Her father had never been a part of her life, and her mother was a chronic alcoholic. So her grandparents raised her in line with their traditional beliefs. "My grandmother would teach me to do things and say, 'This is how you vacuum for a man,'" recalls Genesis. They were puzzled by Genesis, who, at eighteen, had never been on a date with a boy. Her grandparents had no inkling that Genesis had been dating a girl, a twenty-five-year-old coworker from her part-time job at a home improvement store.

Rumors swirled around her high school about why she didn't date. One day, toward the end of her senior year, a boy in her class was ribbing Genesis for sitting close beside one of her female friends. "What are you? Gay?" he taunted. Her reply startled even herself: "Actually, I am."

Word travels fast in a small southern town. The grapevine whispered to her grandparents about the girlfriend. They threatened to have Genesis's twenty-five-year-old girlfriend arrested for statutory rape if she didn't end the relationship. Genesis moved out of her grandparents' house three days after her high school graduation.

Life wasn't easy on her own. She tried a semester of community college but dropped out. She found another girlfriend, whom Genesis describes as verbally abusive, and she worked a series of unsatisfying jobs. Lying on the couch one day, home sick from work, she saw a casting call on MTV for *Real World*. To Genesis, it looked like a ticket out of her relationship, her job, and Mississippi. "It looked good to someone who was twenty and broke," says Genesis.

For Genesis, *Real World* was a great experience—until she watched it on television. She loved living in Boston with her *Real World* housemates and seeing a new part of the country. But the packaging of the show was a disappointment to her. "The experience I lived and what you see on TV are very different," she said. "They take six months of footage and create twenty-two-minute episodes that aren't even in chronological order." The drama surrounding her was whether she would fall for a male cross-dresser on the show. The show leads the viewer to conclude that she did. Genesis just laughs and shakes her head.

In the wake of *Real World*, Genesis accepted invitations to speak on college campuses about her reality-television experience. She had hoped it would give her an opportunity to also talk to students about gay rights and AIDS issues. But she found the students were always interested in the same thing. "They only wanted to talk about *Real World*," she says.

Genesis relates these stories of coming out and the wedge it created between her and her grandparents in a calm, matter-of-fact manner—almost as if she is describing something that happened to someone else. Her focus is on the here and now. The past can't bring her any happiness, but the present and the future can. She has mended her relationship with her grandfather. She even told him about her first marriage to Paige. Her grandfather was calm and wished her well, but he discouraged Genesis from telling her grandmother. "Let's just keep this between us," he said.

Since she was eighteen, Genesis has been comfortable with being public about her sexuality. For Beth, it's a luxury that has only come with financial security. "I knew the day I would be able to be gay was the day I was financially independent," says Beth.

She grew up in New York City in a middle-class family. But she rubbed elbows with many financially fortunate people. From a young age, Beth was impressed by the power of appearances. She moved to California at twenty-two, armed with a degree in marketing from Long Island University and a passion for the fitness business. She began to study yoga in California and was struck by how poorly traditional yoga fit in to the health club setting. That led her to create her own brand of yoga, which combined the poses and rhythms she loved with the faster pace of the health club environment.

During her twenties, Beth was involved in a long-term relationship with a man. But at twenty-nine, she fell in love with a woman for the first time. Her business was beginning to gel, but she was hesitant to be "out" for fear of jeopardizing YogaFit.

With a well-established business to her credit, Beth is now beginning to feel comfortable taking Genesis to industry events. They attend some awards and fitness business dinners together, and Genesis travels to conferences and training seminars with Beth. Genesis also does graphic design work for the company and manages the studio. "I still have a concern it could affect my business," Beth admits.

Her business has begun to contribute to gay and lesbian causes, last year supporting Lambda Legal, and Beth is growing increasingly incensed that her relationship with Genesis doesn't receive the same status as heterosexual marriages. "I have no complaints about my life. My relationship has not hurt me," says Beth. "Except when it comes to getting the same rights and benefits as other people who are not contributing as much. I own a successful business. I pay a fortune in taxes. Why can't I get the same rights as every other taxpayer? It's liberty and justice for all, unless society doesn't support your choice of partnership."

Beth works hard, and she has woven the concept of giving back to society into the fabric of her company. She requires all her fitness trainers to devote eight hours of community service work each year to teaching yoga to people who wouldn't normally have access to it—such as women who are survivors of domestic violence, people who are recovering from cancer, or underprivileged children. "I want to make a difference," Beth says. Eyeing her two dogs, who have hidden themselves under the terrace table, she adds that her biggest pet causes are animal-related, especially supporting animal rescue.

Beth comes from a small family. Her father passed away and her mother has moved to Los Angeles to become a part of the YogaFit business. The core of Beth's and Genesis's family now is a circle of close friends, a few same-sex couples in Palm Springs, and their dear friend Luis Cepeda. He's a fitness instructor, originally from Venezuela, whom Beth met while she was training YogaFit teachers in Turkey. He's become a part of their family, accompanying them to Palm Springs to soak up the desert sun and to date some men Beth and Genesis set him up with. His tan, sculpted body is featured in YogaFit's marketing materials, and Luis is one of the trainers working out in the Palm Springs yoga video. "Women love Luis," Beth says, commenting on the devoted following of straight women that she often sees gay fitness instructors attract.

Back at the video shoot, Beth and Luis, in matching black yoga pants and tank tops, follow the outline of exercises that Beth has written on large sheets of construction paper and duct-taped to a palm tree. The photographer Genesis chats with is another *Real World* veteran, Norman Korpi. He was the first gay character on the show's first season in New York in 1992. He has become a film producer, writer, and director; his first feature film, *The Wedding Video*, released in 2001, spoofs the reality-television genre in a soap opera–like story of the events leading up to a gay wedding.

In this backyard, and in much of Palm Springs, the crowd assembled for the video shoot is more gay than straight, and that's just the way Beth likes it. "Beth has been living for so long in straight society that she likes to be in an all-gay neighborhood," says Genesis. Beth smiles, revealing two rows of straight, white teeth, and says, "It's nice to be in a place where people point and say things like, 'That's the house with the straight couple.'"

Whether Beth and Genesis are together in a primarily gay or straight group, they're hopeful that they can be a force of social change through their financial support of causes they believe in and through the healing power of yoga exercise and the spirituality it brings with it. The words Beth uses during the exercise video to motivate her viewers are also words to live by: "Use the breath to move our bodies," she encourages. "Find more space physically and more space mentally. Challenge yourself to feel a little bit more."

Jonathan and Dean

"We'll keep getting married until it takes."

D ean Backus never imagined that at age thirty-eight he would be contemplating his third marriage. Nor did his partner, forty-one-year-old Jonathan Thalberg. They take some comfort in knowing that all their marriages have been to each other. And they agree that they're going to keep getting married until the vows really stick. In their own eyes, their lives are joined. Dean and Jonathan are just waiting for the laws to catch up.

The first wedding, witnessed by 170 family members and friends, was an elaborate, elegant ceremony with a garden reception in San Jose, California, in October 2000. They had taken three years to plan it, considering every detail from the color of the linen napkins to a hayride for the guests. An Episcopal priest conducted the ceremony, which concluded with Jonathan and Dean vowing their love and fidelity by signing a traditional Jewish *ketubah*, or marriage agreement. Jonathan and Dean called it a marriage. The Episcopal Church, however, called it a blessing of their relationship.

Their second wedding was in a San Francisco City Hall corridor in February 2004. Jonathan and Dean made an impromptu decision to join the more than four thousand other same-sex couples reveling in the Winter of Love after Mayor Gavin Newsome instructed city officials to license gay marriages.

Jonathan and Dean drove up to San Francisco on Sunday, February 15, and joined the line of couples snaking around the plaza in front of City Hall. After five hours, they were turned away by weary clerks, who had been issuing a continuous stream of same-sex marriage licenses for four days. City Hall was closed the next day for Presidents' Day, but on Tuesday morning, Jonathan and Dean arose in their San Jose condominium at 2:00 in the morning to beat the marriage rush. Dean was suffering from a horrible cold and would happily have stayed in bed. "I saw from the look in Jonathan's eye that this was very important to him," says Dean. He fortified himself with cough syrup and got in the car.

They passed almost no one on the freeway driving north, but when they reached San Francisco at 3:30, couples were already in line, brave souls who had camped out overnight. Jonathan and Dean joined the queue with their lawn chairs, a thermos of hot cocoa, and a deck of cards. With them were their friends Theo and Dio, another couple intent on legal same-sex marriage.

Dean and Jonathan

Clerks arrived at 8:00 and passed out numbers to the waiting couples, who were now being sprinkled by an increasingly steady rain. Jonathan and Dean were numbers nineteen and twenty. Supporters gathered, passing out flowers, coffee and donuts, and bottled water. By 9:00, Jonathan and Dean advanced into the building for the indoor portion of their wait. Two hours later, they were at the window of the clerk's office, signing the paperwork they had been seeking together for nearly ten years. With pens in one hand and cell phones in the other, they each called their parents, Dean's in Seattle and Jonathan's in Los Angeles, and were heralded with cheers and good wishes from them all. They waited for Theo and Dio to complete their licenses, and then the four men walked down the corridor to be greeted by a rush of well-wishers and a squadron of judges, clerks, and ministers waiting to perform on-the-spot weddings. They settled on a minister named Liza—that's all they remember of her name—and picked a spot under a massive clock outside Mayor Newsome's office. "We liked the symbolism of the clock," says Dean. "It said to us, 'It's time.'"

It took just fifteen minutes for Liza to marry Jonathan and Dean, as Theo and Dio witnessed, and then to wed Theo and Dio, as Jonathan and Dean looked on. As much as they all would have liked to linger through the vows, they also wanted to make way for the crush of marriage hopefuls behind them. Fatigue was also setting in, and Dean's cough syrup was wearing off. It was noon, almost nine hours after they had lined up in the rain for their marriage license. The foursome set off for a wedding lunch at San Francisco's beloved Zuni Café, where the waiters served them free champagne. Then Jonathan drove to work in Silicon Valley, and Dean went home to bed. They were married men.

For weeks afterward, their mailbox was stuffed. Friends and family sent cards of love and congratulations. And so did department stores, mortgage companies, and travel agencies eager to arrange a honeymoon. They were part of the newest, hottest target audience for direct-mail advertising.

Just six months after their wedding, however, an unwelcome, impersonal, and bureaucratic letter dropped through the mail slot. Following a decision by the California Supreme Court, all the same-sex marriages—including theirs—had been invalidated. The letter told them that in the eyes of the State of California, they were single men again. "It was devastating," Jonathan recalls. "People can't seem to get it through their heads that you can't put restrictions on a couple just because they're not the standard cake top." Jonathan was angry and hurt for days. He fixated on a television show about a Las Vegas wedding chapel where people wandered in to get married on a whim. "That wasn't showing me the sanctity of marriage," Jonathan glowers. "Two strangers could walk into that chapel off the street and get married, and they would have more rights than we do."

Dean surprised himself by the calm with which he accepted the invalidation. "I focused on this as a civil rights issue, and that we have a few more days to tote the weary load. But we shall overcome," he says optimistically.

Ever persistent, Jonathan and Dean are hoping that the third time is the charm. They're keeping a close eye on Dean's home state of Washington. If same-sex marriage becomes legal there, they will try again. "We'll keep getting married until it takes," says Dean. "It doesn't feel like a radical thing to do. It just feels natural."

Jonathan and Dean complement each other. They're burly men of slightly varying shades. Dean has reddish-blond hair and a beard, while Jonathan is clean-shaven with dark brown hair receding slightly at the temples. In some gay circles, they would be labeled "bears," large, stocky white men who favor the comfort of T-shirts and work boots over fashion and fitness. They didn't realize they were part of a trend for many years. "It's something we've drifted into, but we're comfortable with it," says Dean. "The tenet of the 'bear' thing is that you don't have to spend eight hours a day in the gym and be plucked and wear designer labels. It's a natural thing."

If the story of Dean and Jonathan's meeting were written in a movie script—something that Dean, a screenwriter, might do someday—it would be too corny to be produced and stereotypical to the point of political incorrectness.

They met at a Bette Midler concert in San Francisco on New Year's Eve 1993 at ten minutes to midnight. They were both attending as volunteer ushers. Their eyes met during intermission and lingered on each other long enough to convey mutual interest. After the concert, Jonathan and Dean had a picture taken together in front of a Bette Midler poster in the theater lobby. Jonathan gave Dean his card and told him to call him if he wanted a copy. Dean definitely wanted a copy. "Jonathan was the paradigm of what I like: dark hair, a little stocky, not too tall. And he had big, brown, puppy-dog eyes," he says. It is an archetype that has appealed to Dean his entire life. "My first crush at age seven was on Paul Bunyan," he concedes, and laughs. "That's still the kind of guy I like, just slightly shorter!"

Dean called Jonathan a few days later, and that week they went on their first official date. They fell for each other quickly. Nine months later, Dean moved into Jonathan's San Jose apartment, and they have been together ever since.

They've weathered the marriage roller coaster together, and a career roller coaster as well. Both lost their jobs in the high-tech world of Silicon Valley after the dot-com bust. Dean took his layoff as a chance to leave the business world and pursue high school teaching and screenwriting. Jonathan opened a gourmet shop called "It's Delicious!" He cultivated a devoted following over three years, purveying teas and olives, chutneys and chocolates. But faced with the choice between expanding the business or closing it, Jonathan decided to shutter his store and found his way back into the corporate world as a middle manager of computer programmers.

Dean hasn't followed Jonathan back into high-tech. He has worked for three years as a substitute teacher, using his afternoons and summers off to polish his screenplays. He was recently invited to submit three to Paramount Pictures—the lucky offshoot of his second-place finish in the national finals of a television game show. In the summer of 2004, Dean appeared on *The Ultimate Film Fanatic*, a game show on the IFC cable network. The competition pits movie buffs against each other in the categories of movie trivia and film debates. There's even a round in which obsessive movie fans compete to show who has more and better movie memorabilia. Dean captured the western U.S. regional title, and in the show's final episode, came within one spot of clinching the national title. In addition to $5,000 and a big-screen plasma television, Dean won a chance to have his screenplays reviewed by a Paramount Pictures producer.

Jonathan and Dean share a passion for food—a love that flourished during Jonathan's "It's Delicious" period—and for film. Their condo is a two-level shrine to all things Hollywood, especially all things Disney. Winnie the Pooh statues, Wizard of Oz figurines, ET toys, a Peter Pan mobile, and a Han Solo action figure, still in the box. A series of framed prints by Hawaiian artist Jim Kingwell are scattered throughout their home. They are tranquil, colorful, light-hearted reminders of the couple's eight-day honeymoon in Hawaii.

Over their fireplace hangs one of the few decorative items in their house that isn't whimsical. It is their ornate ketubah, a solemn but joyous framed memory of their first wedding. Though Jonathan converted to Episcopalianism after meeting Dean, he was raised Jewish and considers himself "an Episcopalian Jew." Jonathan calls the Episcopal teaching "just another layer on my faith." He sums up his faith succinctly: "I believe in acceptance and compassion."

Jonathan's mother has a different idea of faith, however, and was slow to warm to the idea of an Episcopal wedding for her only son. "She had more trouble with me being an Episcopalian than with me being a boy," says Dean.

Dean's mother helped bring Jonathan's mother peace about a Christian wedding. The two mothers didn't meet until the day before the wedding, although they did talk on the phone to discuss which family members should be in which wedding pictures and—of course—what to wear. Dean remembers his mother calling him after an hour-and-a-half conversation with his mother-in-law-to-be, saying, "Judy is such a nice lady, but she is so sad. Isn't there something Jewish you can do for the ceremony?"

Not long after that exchange, Jonathan and Dean attended a traditional Jewish wedding between a man and a woman. During the signing of the ketubah, an idea dawned on both of them. Not only did they arrange to have a handsome ketubah made for their own wedding but they had it matted and framed, and they appointed Judy the ketubah's keeper. It was her job to ensure that each guest signed the border of the ketubah. For Jonathan and Dean, it was an ideal way to weave Jonathan's heritage prominently into their union. For Judy, it was a *mitzvah*—a blessing and a good deed.

Being film buffs and foodies, Jonathan and Dean's wedding and reception were staged with all the care and grandeur of a Hollywood production. They took three years to plan the wedding. That gave Jonathan time to complete his M.B.A. and allowed them both to obsess over every detail of the day they called "The Big Event."

Guests received a three-page "Save the Date" letter in advance of their invitations. In a cheeky, question-and-answer format, Jonathan and Dean provided a glimpse of the upcoming spectacle. In the letter's list of Frequently Asked Questions, they even answered the question, "I've never been to a commitment ceremony before. What can I expect?" Their answer? "Most of the things you'd find at a heterosexual wedding, aside from no chick in a white dress and no bouquets. Other than that, it's pretty standard stuff. (You may be more at sea with it being an Episcopal service than a gay one.)" Another question: "Which of you is the bride and will you wear a dress?" Their answer: "If you are seriously asking this question, don't come."

The ceremony was at the Trinity Episcopal Cathedral, a Victorian Gothic church in downtown San Jose. Dean's sisters, Emily and Sara, and Jonathan's sister Susanne were all proudly in attendance, and each did readings during the hour-long ceremony. After her brief shock at the church—with its large crosses and depictions of Jesus Christ—Jonathan's mother tended to the ketubah. Dean's parents and Jonathan's father were there as well, to witness their sons, in matching black suits and burgundy shirts, walking up the aisle hand-in-hand, in love.

The reception was at a historic Victorian mansion with manicured gardens and an expansive lawn that was scattered with dining tables. The reception was draped in harvest colors, with burgundy, orange, red, and forest green linens, piles of pumpkins and bougainvilleas, shafts of wheat, and bowls of pomegranates and persimmons. Jonathan had contracted with California wineries to collect a variety of wine labels to use as place cards. Their cake was a three-tiered masterpiece in butter cream, decorated with grapes and vines. On the highest layer was a custom-made cake top, a gift they saw for the first time on their wedding day.

Their dear friend Pats had insisted for months that she would supply the cake top. The night before the wedding, she disappointed Jonathan and Dean by showing them a fake cake top—two male dolls in Hawaiian shirts that she had gotten from a Jack in the Box fast-food restaurant and glued to a base. Jonathan and Dean thought it was hideous and struggled to disguise their dislike. The next day, when they saw their cake, they knew they'd been had. Pats's real cake top was Peter Pan, Dean's favorite Disney character, sitting on a miniature bale of hay beside Winnie the Pooh, Jonathan's favorite. It was their ideal centerpiece for the day.

The reception lasted for seven hours. A caricaturist roamed the grounds sketching guests. Friends toasted and roasted them at an open mike. Their friend Dustin got the night's biggest laughs when he called on everyone in the crowd "with a key to Dean's love shack to please come forward and turn it in." Nearly all the men at the wedding got up, walked to the microphone, and dropped off a key. Next Dustin asked "anyone with a key to Jonathan's love shack to please come forward and drop off the key." This time, all the women came up, as Dean and Jonathan laughed until they were breathless. As the testimonials wound down, the DJ arrived to play their first dance to the song "That's All," with Johnny Mathis crooning, ""I can only give you love that lasts forever and the promise to be near each time you call."

The day was a miracle for them. After a week of torrential rains, the skies had cleared to a warm and sunny Northern California autumn afternoon. Friends and family had gathered from up and down the West Coast. David, a high school friend of Jonathan's, initially said he would come to the reception but wouldn't set foot in a church for a gay wedding as a staunch Catholic: "I can't. I don't support it." Roundly chastised by Jonathan's brother-in-law, David did attend the ceremony. He was so moved that by the time the dancing started, he cut in on a dance between Jonathan and Dean so he could dance with Jonathan at his wedding. During their dance, David told Jonathan, "I'm glad I came."

Dean and Jonathan have more than a rapport. They have shtick, a steady banter of movie lines and jokes. Even when they compliment each other, there's a bit of stand-up comedy in the air.

"You're my role model," says Jonathan to Dean.

"You're *my* role model," Dean shoots back, launching a playful argument over which of them is more compassionate.

But behind their movie obsessions and humor, a serious side surfaces when they discuss topics like gay rights. Jonathan gets close to anger when he talks about the illegality of same-sex marriage. "Anybody should be able to love anybody, and it's not okay when people tell us that just because the person you love is of the same gender, then it's not okay. Why does sexual orientation make a difference? Marriage is simply a contract that says, 'I'm responsible for you, and you're responsible for me.' The government needs to be focusing on governing, not on morality." Just as quickly as he's worked himself into a fit of pique, Jonathan begins to wind down. "I'm hopeful that in our lifetime, we'll see that *different* does not equal wrong."

Dean is quieter during discussions of their rights. He's more prone to write about them than debate them. He has woven gay themes into his screenplays and his short stories. And the tragedy of Matthew Shepard, the twenty-one-year-old man who was murdered in an anti-gay hate crime in Laramie, Wyoming, inspired him to poetry. In a poem he calls "Just Like Matthew," Dean wrote,

I am a gay man
Just like Matthew

I am an Episcopalian
Just like Matthew

I am a Sagittarius
Just like Matthew

I am short and blond
Just like Matthew

I love soccer, dancing, and theater
Just like Matthew

I spoke three languages
Just like Matthew

I want to make the world a better place
Just like Matthew

I trust people at face value
Just like Matthew

I give my love and friendship to people
Just like Matthew

I know how to cry
Just like Matthew

And on Monday October 12th 1998
With a last shuddering gasp
As one last star fell
Part of me died
Just like Matthew.

Unlike Matthew, Dean got the chance to marry the man he loved, even if the state recognized it only for a fleeting six months.

There is one enduring benefit of Jonathan's and Dean's San Francisco marriage that lives on. They still have family car insurance.

Jonathan had long been frustrated that he and Dean were unable to get an auto insurance policy together. The difference between insurance for a married couple and for two single people was costing them more than $300 each year. Jonathan had debated with his insurance carrier several times after their San Jose wedding, arguing that they were entitled to a joint policy. Each time, however, the insurer turned him down because he and Dean weren't legally married.

The day after their San Francisco wedding, Jonathan faxed off a copy of their marriage license to their insurance company. They qualified for the married rate at last. The city of San Francisco may have voided their marriage, but Jonathan hasn't notified their car insurance carrier. So even if they don't sense marriage rights at other times, at least when they drive, Jonathan and Dean feel legally married.

They talk often now of packing up and leaving the Bay Area, with its crowds, traffic, and high cost of living. Oregon is where they would most likely go, even though the Oregon weddings that took place alongside the San Francisco ones during the winter of 2004 have also been voided by the courts.

Jonathan and Dean are hoping that the State of Washington Supreme Court will legalize same-sex marriages. If that happens, they'll head up there for wedding number three. They've already narrowed the location down to two sites—the medieval-style chapel at St. Paul's Cathedral in Seattle or a small chapel in the Tacoma woods on the campus of Dean's high school. And if the legality of that marriage falls through, Jonathan and Dean will start making plans again.

Jill and Vickie

*"I don't know what it's like
not to have two moms."*

For seventeen years, Vickie Riggs was openly welcomed at her partner Jill Selleck's family events. If Vickie didn't make the trek to northeastern Pennsylvania for birthdays or celebrations, Jill's family missed her and wondered why Jill hadn't brought her "roommate" along.

That inclusiveness came to an abrupt and unforeseen end for Jill and Vickie in 1994. They had mailed Jill's family joyful letters announcing that Vickie was pregnant, along with copies of the book *Heather Has Two Mommies*. Their excitement over the coming baby was dowsed by a torrent of disapproval. Outraged, two of Jill's siblings returned the books with irate letters, and one of her nieces sent the book back to Jill in tatters. One of her siblings insisted that Vickie belonged to a cult and begged Jill to leave her and come home to the family farm. Jill's mother suffered a heart attack, and her siblings shunned Jill when she drove down to the hospital. Jill's father stopped speaking to her.

While Jill was visiting her sick mother, Vickie was home opening the unwelcome letters from Jill's family. "I didn't want to pick up the phone or bring in the mail," she recalls. "It was just hate coming in waves."

"This was the family that I had always told Vickie would take care of us," recalls Jill. She had listened in disbelief as Vickie read the letters over the phone. "I don't think I really believed what I was hearing until I returned to our home in New Jersey and read the letters myself."

Despite the invitation to return to the dairy farm she had left two decades before, Jill stayed by Vickie's side at their home in Maplewood, New Jersey, and together they welcomed Richard, a towheaded baby boy, into their family. Richard has grown into a slender, precocious ten-year-old, big brother to Clay, eight years old. Together they play soccer and video games, growing up as "normal boys," even though that is exactly what Jill's family had predicted they could never become, being raised by two mothers. "My biological family is two hundred miles and forty years away," says Jill. She grows tearful over the loss of her relationship with the family she grew up in, but she admits that the sadness has mellowed over time. Together for twenty-eight years, Jill and

Jill, Vickie, Richard and Clay

Vickie have diverted their energies toward their own family. Life with two active boys doesn't leave a lot of time for mourning the loss of bitter family members. And the two women harness any extra vigor they have to advocate for families like theirs.

Vickie and Jill have drawn on a growing network of same-sex parents to create a loving community for themselves and their sons. They are both committed activists, working to raise awareness of discrimination against families headed by same-sex partners. Says Vickie, "We're very much aware that we're role models. Sometimes we don't want to always be the head lesbians. But we have to be." Vickie laughs, breaking into a broad smile that lights up her green eyes. Faint laugh lines underscore her gentle sense of humor.

When Vickie, now forty-nine, and Jill, now fifty-three, decided that they wanted to start a family, they didn't know that they were on the cusp of a "gayby boom"—a sharp increase in same-sex parents having children. They've raised their boys among a community of progressive gay families; there are more than fifty same-sex-parented families with children in their boys' school district. Even though the scars left by Jill's family remain, the couple has been heartened by the support of other gay families and a growing acceptance from the community at large. "Maplewood has a diversity of culture, race, and family constellations," says Jill. "This diversity is the reason that we were attracted to the town—along with the housing stock of turn-of-the-century homes." Jill and Vickie lobbied hard for community acceptance, and despite the demands of their own family life, along with medical battles that both Jill and Vickie have faced, neither shows any sign that they will give up the fight for equal treatment.

"I get angry at any queer family that's not putting their resources toward civil rights," says Jill, her gaze intense behind her rectangular black-frame glasses. "I want everyone to step up."

Jill's and Vickie's lives have demanded that they be trailblazing and ordinary, untraditional and traditional, all at the same time. Protests and activism have become routine, but most of their days are consumed by the quotidian demands of suburban parenting.

Vickie is the family breadwinner. She works as a fiber-optics engineer. And Jill, much to her own surprise, is a stay-at-home mom. It's not a choice either of these two committed feminists could have imagined making before Richard and Clay entered their lives. Vickie took umbrage during her pregnancy any time someone presumptuously asked whether she would be returning to work after the baby was born. She never imagined why anyone would do otherwise. Jill presumed she would always be working as well. "When I was working, I had no respect for stay-at-home mothers," says Jill. But the course of life, particularly when children are involved, has a way of changing even one's staunchest convictions.

Jill took a year off work after Richard was born. She had spent two decades as the proprietor of a gift and flower shop, but she returned to the mental health field after Richard was born. She worked as a liaison between state-run mental health facilities and a private nonprofit provider of residential homes for people with mental illness. While at that job, Jill underwent minor outpatient surgery, which seemed successful. Within a week, she was back at work but her condition was deteriorating fast. She picked up Richard from day care one day and found she was so short of breath she could barely walk up their short driveway. Jill locked the baby-gate across Richard's playroom and lay on the floor until Vickie could get home from work. She had developed a pulmonary embolism, a blood clot in her lungs. One of her lungs stopped functioning completely. By the time she reached the emergency room, only two-thirds of the other lung was working, and it was fading fast. Jill recalls one doctor in the intensive-care unit asking her, "Why are you alive?"

Doctors intervened in the nick of time and treated the blood clot successfully. The psychological impact of the experience wasn't quite so fleeting for Vickie and Jill. "It's a mind-altering experience when you could have been dead," says Jill. "It gave me a lot to think about." She examined her life and realized there were two things she wanted: "I wanted to build a stone wall, and I wanted to be with Richard." Jill is an artistic woman who works well with her hands. She crafts mosaics and pottery. She's built radiator covers in their sunny colonial home and a network of her stone walls terraces their gently sloping yard. After staring death in the face, Jill decided her artistic temperament was better suited to caring for her child and her home. And she soon realized it would also give her more time to work for equality. "Building these stone walls was preparing me to begin to do the work I needed to do for the family's basic civil rights," says Jill.

Jill has been active in the town's Parent Teacher Association and has served on the board of the Family Pride Coalition, a national advocacy group that supports lesbian, gay, bisexual, and transgender parents and their families. She has helped arrange exhibits about diverse families and supported the high school's gay-straight alliance.

The couple has been heartened by the power of efforts in Maplewood to move the cause of same-sex families forward. One panel discussion in particular showed them how far society has come since they were teenagers hiding their sexuality. A high school student on the panel told the audience how moved she was to meet so many queer parents and that as a young lesbian she was glad to learn she could have a family someday. It's a sign of progress and enlightenment to Vickie and Jill, giving them hope that one day the higher rates of suicide, depression, and drug abuse among gay and lesbian teens will abate. Acceptance and openness, they know, are the only way to make that happen.

For every successful panel discussion and photo exhibit, there's at least one battle that needs waging—and usually more. In one instance, a flyer announcing a panel discussion that was sent home from school with the children ignited a war of words among parents. Some were outraged that a paper with the words "gay, lesbian, and transgender" was mixed in with their children's homework assignments. Vickie and Jill are under no illusions that their advocacy work is done.

"Having kids, you don't get to decide if you're going to come out or not," says Vickie. Clay and Richard spread the word in the normal course of their conversations and interactions with their friends. This became abundantly clear to Vickie and Jill when Richard went out trick-or-treating when he was four. Proudly dressed in his Halloween costume, Richard marched up to ring doorbells in search of candy. Neighbors would smile and ask what he was. "I am a knight," he said, beaming. "And I have two moms."

Maplewood is a leafy suburb twenty miles from Manhattan. Children ride their bikes along the wide sidewalks as jogging parents in New York Yankees caps follow closely behind. The quaint downtown is full of day spas and coffee shops, toy stores and book shops, an artsy movie theater, and real estate firms marketing half-million-dollar Colonial homes.

It's an idyllic setting Vickie and Jill never could have imagined when they met at a party in 1977, both so poor they would budget their groceries down to the last penny. Mutual friends introduced them at a party in Pittsburgh. Vickie was twenty-one and aimless. She had left her New Hampshire home to go to Keene State College but dropped out, preferring to wander around the country, sometimes hitchhiking from one friend's house to the next, other times working odd jobs in an effort to find herself. At twenty-five, Jill looked like the picture of stability to Vickie. She had a steady job at a florist, and she had a car. That October night, they both felt drawn to each other. "I was instantly attracted to her," remembers Vickie. Jill says, "I remember looking into those green eyes and thinking I had met this person before. I felt like there was already a connection."

They talked for hours until Jill had to leave to drive a friend to Erie. It seemed natural to Jill to ask Vickie to come along. "I was really upset when Jill said she had to leave. So when she asked me to come along, I said yes," Vickie recalls. "I figured I'd never see her again." The drive only increased their interest in each other. And three months later, Vickie moved in with Jill in Pennsylvania.

"We know we're just like the old joke about lesbians," says Vickie, recounting the well-worn cliché with a laugh. "What does a lesbian bring on her second date? A U-Haul!" Neither could imagine that a long-distance relationship would work. So they got an apartment together not far from Jill's family farm. Scrimping pennies together, both women went back to college. Jill attended night school to earn a degree in accounting while she worked in the flower shop. And Vickie drove fifty miles each way to the State University of New York at Binghamton to earn a bachelor's degree in chemistry. After they moved to New Jersey, Vickie also completed a master's in chemistry at Rutgers.

Vickie's colleagues in fiber-optics engineering have been almost exclusively men. She's open now about her family at work, but it has taken her a long time to get to that point. At some jobs, she would make up stories about having a boyfriend, but usually she just didn't talk about her personal life at all. "People thought I was unfriendly," she says. "I was very discreet."

But just as Richard and Clay have outed their moms, it's virtually impossible for Vickie and Jill not to talk about their children. There's no way for a slender woman like Vickie to hide a pregnancy. And in 2000, Vickie took time away from work to make a journey to Asia to adopt Clay, then three, and bring him back to Maplewood as a new and treasured member of their family.

Vickie and Jill are so much like other families—gay or straight—that they find their straight friends often don't understand their limited rights. "We have good friends who assume that because we act like a family we have all the rights of a family," says Jill. Vickie and Jill do have domestic partnership status in New Jersey, and Jill is covered by the health insurance Vickie's employer provides. But Jill has to pay income tax on that health insurance benefit. They paid more than $6,000 in legal fees for Jill to have a second-parent adoption of both their sons. And they can't even get a family auto insurance discount for Jill to drive their second car, so both cars are insured only in Vickie's name.

"We're much more like other families than we are different," says Vickie. "One friend says we should go on TV to show people in the red states how we're just like them. But I told them, 'We can't do that! We're too boring!'"

Jill nods her agreement, raising her eyebrows beneath her gray spiky hair. "The only difference between us and other families is we're pushing to have the same rights."

Clay is clear on what a family is. "A family helps each other," he says. "If one of them gets hurt, they come as fast as they can to help the other one."

Two years older than his brother, Richard tackles a definition of homophobia. "When people are afraid of gays and lesbians, it's called homophobia. I wish people weren't afraid. Gays and lesbians are people who love someone of the same sex. My teacher talks about families. I wish she could talk about my family."

Richard had a year in school when his teacher wouldn't allow him to talk about having two moms. It was devastating for Vickie and Jill, who had always worked so hard in his school—even in his preschool—to expose children to diverse families. It was devastating for Richard too.

The incident stemmed from a special project Jill was organizing to bring portraits of diverse families into the schools through the "Love Makes a Family" program. She vetted the project with the superintendent, the principals, and the PTA, which wanted to see every word of every description of every family. There was resistance from families along the way who said they didn't want their elementary-school-aged children exposed to same-sex couples and to sex. But Jill pushed ahead, primarily for the sake of Richard, who was excited by the prospect of his own family being among the subjects of the beautiful black-and-white photographs. "There is no description of sex or sexuality in the photos," says Jill, who grows frustrated with critics who believe the show is about sex. "It is same-sex parents in the context of their families."

The text that accompanied the photo of the Riggs-Selleck family included Richard's comment that his teacher wouldn't let him talk about his family. That comment was putting the entire project at risk. Jill was astounded that she was being accused of creating the whole exhibit just to get that one line in the show. Ultimately, the school told her the exhibit could only run if their family was not represented in it.

Reluctantly, Jill agreed. But that left the awful job of telling Richard that his family picture wouldn't be there. "He was so proud about this exhibit," says Jill. "But I had to tell him that we wouldn't be in it."

Even more painful than slights such as this one from the community are the slights that come from family. With the exception of her mother, Jill's family has not come to accept her and her children. But Jill's mother died in 2001. "She knew that I was a good person, even though I was a lesbian," says Jill, remembering with tears in her eyes how her mother, seventy-one and in ill health, drove two hundred miles alone after Richard was born to visit her baby grandson. Now Jill has contact with her family only if she initiates it, something she does less and less often.

Jill never could have imagined she would grow so distant from her family. "My childhood was spent celebrating memorable occasions with my aunts, uncles, grandparents, and cousins, 85 percent of whom lived within two miles of our six hundred–acre farm," she recalls. "While other families were involved in our lives, I clearly got the message that my birth family was and always would be my support system. I have wonderful childhood memories of being two and three and sitting on my dad's lap as he drove the farm tractor through the fields. I remember singing our song, 'I love my Daddy,' and then he would respond, 'I love my Jill.'"

Vickie has fared better with her family, though she hasn't felt complete acceptance. Her mother has accepted her for thirty years. After Vickie came out to her over the phone, Vickie's mother rode a bus from Manchester, New Hampshire, to Pittsburgh to show her support. Her father was slower to come around at first, but with the encouragement of Vickie's stepmother, he began to attend Parents and Friends of Lesbians and Gays meetings and has become a doting grandfather. "Now he is extremely supportive," says Vickie. "For many years, he has been our tireless advocate."

Vickie's brother has rejected her. Like Jill's family, Vickie's brother and his wife seemed to change their attitudes toward Jill and Vickie overnight. For years, Jill and Vickie had been loving aunts to their niece, Katie, taking her to museums and indulging her with souvenirs. But when Katie was nine, Vickie's brother decided that Vickie and Jill might be a bad influence on his daughter and might encourage her to become a lesbian. "We racked our brains over what we had done and whether we had ever been inappropriate with her," says Vickie. Her brother assured them that they had not been but that there would be no contact none-theless—at least until Katie turned twenty. Katie is twenty-four now, and Vickie could, theoretically, have contact with her. But the relationship has been lost.

Jill and Vickie have mourned this and other lost family rela-tionships, but their bigger focus by far is the relationships that en-dure. In 2002, they marked their twenty-fifth year together with a grand "Family Celebration." More than a hundred friends and family members gathered at their church, a Unitarian Universalist fellowship in nearby Montclair. Jill hesitates to call it a wedding, because a wedding comes with rights that they don't have. But it was an elaborate recognition of their lives together before the many people who love them. Richard and Clay walked up the aisle together in front of Vickie and Jill. Their minister, Charles Blustein Ortman, along with Vickie's aunt, Judith Walker Riggs, who is also a Unitarian Universalist minister, performed the cer-emony with great enthusiasm.

Two years later, Reverend Ortman was asked to perform a same-sex wedding in New Paltz, New York, after the mayor of that town decided to issue same-sex licenses. He later quipped, "I don't perform same-sex marriages. I commit them."

More than twenty years before this public display of their af-fection and commitment, Vickie and Jill had a tiny ceremony in the woods of Pennsylvania. Three of their close friends were there to watch them sing songs, read vows of love, and exchange rings. Back then, they never could have imagined that two women could celebrate their love for each other so publicly. Vickie remembers the first rumblings about same-sex civil marriages in the 1970s and how skeptical she was at the time. "I wondered then, 'What are the chances of being an out lesbian?' Marriage was so far beyond what I could imagine. I thought I'd be happy to take anything."

Contrasting those days with the day of their Family Celebra-tion, Vickie is struck by how far they've come. She tells Jill, "Hav-ing the community support us and believe in us enhances my relationship with you."

Jill agrees, quiet for a moment as she, too, reflects on the progress they've made. But she clearly sees the need to keep pushing for more. She knows there is more ground to cover. "We've got to be out there marketing our families," Jill says. "We need to keep talking—about marriage, and even about divorce."

Vickie and Jill are not about to give up talking any time soon, despite the demands of two children and their homework, their soccer, their baseball, their friends. Vickie's job is taxing, requiring her to leave the house at 8:00 each weekday morning and return at 7:00 most nights. She manages it despite a worsening chronic-pain condition that limits how far she can walk.

Should Vickie and Jill's energy flag, Richard and Clay seemed poised to pick up the cause. Richard has been the master of Provincetown Family Pride Parade. And his friends are quick to correct anyone who says a child can't have two moms. "Yes you can," one said. "Richard does."

Richard clears up any confusion his friends—or adults—might have about how he was born. "A nice man gave us the sperm," he explains. "A doctor put the needle in Mom, and then I was born."

When pressed, Richard can also be a quiet advocate for same-sex marriage. "Civil marriage is important," he says. "So you can see each other in the hospital."

Like most fourth-grade boys, Richard tires of talking to adults. He is anxious to return to playing on his Game Cube with Clay. It's a weekend-only privilege with the electronic toy he and Clay saved for months to buy themselves. Richard also seems weary of explaining the significance of something that's as natural as breathing to him. "It's normal. I don't know what it's like not to have two moms." He shrugs. "Can I go now?"

Both his mothers nod, and Richard disappears around the corner. "I don't think we're any different than other families," Vickie says with a smile.

Epilogue

Marriage equality should matter to all people. In the famous words of Dr. Martin Luther King Jr., "Injustice anywhere is a threat to justice everywhere." When a man cannot visit his partner in the hospital because he is gay, we all suffer. When two women cannot be legal parents of their children because they are lesbians, all children are harmed. When any two lovers cannot proclaim their love in public, all lovers are diminished.

The radical right has argued that same-sex marriages tarnish the sacred union between a man and a woman. But rights denied to one couple are not rights gained for another. Heterosexual marriages suffer when they come at the expense of loving same-sex unions that cannot be validated.

Discrimination against gays and lesbians flourishes, even as some rights are realized. In the wake of Hurricane Katrina, I traveled to Texas and Louisiana to report on the devastation and the recovery efforts. Apocalyptic stories swirled that the hurricane was God's way of emptying the sinful city of New Orleans of its homosexuals. A minister walked me through a crowded Houston convention center being used as a shelter to thousands of families. He was especially watchful for gays and lesbians, worried they would be targets of hatred and—without the legal status of straight families—that they would not receive the same relief benefits.

The stories of love and family in this book are small examples of the very ordinary dreams and struggles of lesbian and gay couples and families. Change the names around, and they are indistinguishable from the people living next door to you. The people included in this book are no more deserving of discrimination than your neighbors.

Yet only one of these couples has a legal marriage. The marriage of Gary Linnell and Richard Chalmers is recognized by only one state. The federal government doesn't recognize it. And the hard-won marriage rights of Massachusetts couples are vulnerable. There's a movement in Massachusetts to put the civil rights of gay couples on a statewide ballot to ask voters to decide whether every person should have the same basic rights.

Dean Backus and Jonathan Thalberg know what it's like to have a legal marriage—like they did in California—and then have it taken away. For gay and lesbian families, a right given is not a right guaranteed. Anne Magro and Heather Finstuen suffered a similar loss when their parental rights were legislated away by the state of Oklahoma.

So many families are struggling privately without the cloak of marriage to protect them and their rights.

The ten couples in this book have put a smiling face on gay marriage. They have the right to smile, even if they do not yet have the legal right to marry. Imagine how much brighter they could beam if their unions were as celebrated in public as they are within the walls of their own homes?

Their love shouldn't have to be political, but as long as they have to fight for their love to be recognized, it will be.

Resources

Below is a list of the some of the resources available to same-gender couples and families across the country. Many of these organizations also have local chapters, which can be found through their national offices or websites. This list is not meant to be an exhaustive list of the many hundreds of organizations working to advance marriage equality and civil rights for gays and lesbians, but it is a starting point for people seeking information. The descriptions of the organizations are in each group's own words.

American Civil Liberties Union (ACLU)

The ACLU is our nation's guardian of liberty. We work daily in courts, legislatures, and communities to defend and preserve the individual rights and liberties guaranteed to every person in this country by the Constitution and laws of the United States. Our job is to conserve America's original civic values—the Constitution and the Bill of Rights.

American Civil Liberties Union
125 Broad Street, 18th Floor
New York, NY 10004
212/549-2585
www.aclu.org

Children of Lesbians and Gays Everywhere (COLAGE)

COLAGE engages, connects, and empowers people to make the world a better place for children of lesbian, gay, bisexual, and transgender parents.

3543 18th Street, #1
San Francisco, CA 94110
415/861-5437
www.colage.org

Family Pride Coalition (FPC)

FPC is a national non-profit organization that has been solely dedicated to equality for lesbian, gay, bisexual, and transgender parents and their families for twenty-five years. Headquartered in Washington, D.C., FPC supports nearly 200 membership-based LGBT parenting groups nationwide with a base of 35,000 supporters.

P.O. Box 65327
Washington, DC 20035
202/331-5015
www.familypride.org

Freedom to Marry

Freedom to Marry is the gay and non-gay partnership working to win marriage equality nationwide. Headed by Evan Wolfson, a leading civil rights advocate and lawyer, Freedom to Marry brings new resources and a renewed context of urgency and opportunity to this social justice movement. Freedom to Marry brings the work of its partner organizations into a larger whole, a shared civil rights campaign that fosters outreach to non-gay allies.

116 West 23rd Street, Suite 500
New York, NY 10011
212/851-8418
www.freedomtomarry.org

Gay and Lesbian Victory Fund

The Gay and Lesbian Victory Fund provides strategic, technical, and financial support to openly LGBT candidates and officials. Since 1991, Victory has successfully helped elect hundreds of openly LGBT candidates to Congress, state legislatures, school boards, city councils, and more.

1705 DeSales Street NW, Suite 500
Washington, DC 20036
202/842-8679
www.victoryfund.org

Gay and Lesbian Alliance Against Defamation (GLAAD)
GLAAD is dedicated to promoting and ensuring fair, accurate, and inclusive representation of people and events in the media as a means of eliminating homophobia and discrimination based on gender identity and sexual orientation.
5455 Wilshire Boulevard, #1500
Los Angeles, CA 90036
323/933-2240
www.glaad.org

Human Rights Campaign
As America's largest gay and lesbian organization, the Human Rights Campaign provides a national voice on gay and lesbian issues. The Human Rights Campaign effectively lobbies Congress, mobilizes grassroots action in diverse communities, invests strategically to elect a fair-minded Congress, and increases public understanding through innovative education and communication strategies.
1640 Rhode Island Avenue NW
Washington, DC 20036
202/628-4160
www.hrc.org

Lambda Legal
Lambda Legal is a national organization committed to achieving full recognition of the civil rights of lesbians, gay men, bisexuals, transgender people, and those with HIV through impact litigation, education, and public policy work.
120 Wall Street, Suite 1500
New York, NY 10005
212/809-8585
www.lambdalegal.org

Log Cabin Republicans
The mission of the Log Cabin Republicans is to work within the Republican Party to advocate equal rights for all Americans, including gays and lesbians. Log Cabin's mission derives from our firm belief in the principles of limited government, individual liberty, individual responsibility, free markets, and a strong national defense. We emphasize that these principles and the moral values

on which they stand are consistent with the pursuit of equal treatment under the law for gay and lesbian Americans.
1607 17th Street NW
Washington, DC 20009
202/347-5306
www.logcabin.org

Marriage Equality USA
The mission of Marriage Equality is to secure the freedom and the right of same-sex couples to enter into a legally recognized civil marriage having all the federal and state benefits and responsibilities which that entails.
P.O. Box 121
Old Chelsea Station
New York, NY 10113
877/571-5729
www.marriageequality.org

National Association of LGBT Community Centers
The National Association of LGBT Community Centers exists to support and enhance lesbian, gay, bisexual, and transgender community centers, which are engines of community organizing and liberation, and crucial to the health and strength of LGBT communities.
1325 Massachusetts Avenue, Suite 600
Washington, DC 20005
202/639-6325
www.lgbtcenters.org

National Black Justice Coalition
The National Black Justice Coalition is a civil rights organization of black lesbian, gay, bisexual, and transgender people and our allies dedicated to fostering equality by fighting racism and homophobia. The Coalition advocates for social justice by educating and mobilizing opinion leaders, including elected officials, clergy, and media, with a focus on black communities.
1725 I Street NW, Suite 300
Washington, DC 20006
202/349-3756
www.nbjcoalition.org

National Center for Lesbian Rights (NCLR)

NCLR is a national legal resource center with a primary commitment to advancing the rights and safety of lesbians and their families through a program of litigation, public policy advocacy, and public education. In addition, NCLR provides representation and resources to gay men and bisexual and transgender individuals on key issues that also significantly advance lesbian rights.

870 Market Street, Suite 370
San Francisco, CA 94102
415/392-6257
www.nclrights.org

National Gay and Lesbian Task Force

Founded in 1973, the National Gay and Lesbian Task Force Foundation was the first national lesbian, gay, bisexual, and transgender civil rights and advocacy organization. It works to build the grassroots political strength of the community by training state and local activists and leaders and organizing broad-based campaigns to defeat anti-LGBT referenda and advance pro-LGBT legislation.

1325 Massachusetts Avenue NW, Suite 600
Washington, DC 20005
202/393-5177
www.thetaskforce.org

National Stonewall Democrats

The National Stonewall Democrats is a grassroots force for social change within the LGBT movement and within the Democratic Party. Our members do the hard work of calling voters, putting together campaign mailings, going door-to-door for fair-minded candidates, and having tough conversations with Democratic party officials about why LGBT families need and deserve more support from the party and its elected officials.

1325 Massachusetts Avenue NW, Suite 700
Washington, DC 20005
202/625-1382
www.stonewalldemocrats.org

OutProud

OutProud, The National Coalition for Gay, Lesbian, Bisexual and Transgender Youth, serves the needs of these young men and women by providing advocacy, information, resources, and support. Our goal is to help queer youth become happy, successful, confident, and vital gay, lesbian, and bisexual adults.

369 3rd Street, Suite B-362
San Rafael, CA 94901
www.outproud.org

Parents, Families and Friends of Lesbians and Gays (PFLAG)

PFLAG promotes the health and well-being of gay, lesbian, bisexual, and transgender persons and their families and friends through support, to cope with an adverse society; education, to enlighten an ill-informed public; and advocacy, to end discrimination and to secure equal civil rights.

1726 M Street NW, Suite 400
Washington, DC 20036
202/467-8180
www.pflag.org

Acknowledgments

This book could not have happened without all the couples and families who opened their hearts and shared their stories. Thanks to them and to the many people who helped me find them: Brandon Braud, Diane Daniel, Alexandra Varney McDonald, and Emily Graham.

Friends around the country opened their homes to me while I was traveling, and I am very grateful to them. They include Graham, Sam, and Daniel Stevens; and the Reverend Elizabeth Stevens, who even preached on hospitality while she hosted me; Diane Daniel and Wessel Kok; and Erik Gundersen and Chan Lee.

The support of my friends has been invaluable. Elaine McArdle's insight, wit, and intelligence have guided me through countless personal and professional thickets. And my dear friends Kathi Pelkey and Mary Schwarzer Hampton have provided assurance, good humor, and long-distance hugs. You are my three muses, who inspire me in different and important ways. Roblyn Brigham and Jenifer Goldman-Fraser, thank you for watching the boys, lending your ears, and always being willing to go for a much-needed run or walk. I'm also indebted to "the girls," Polly and Bubba Bartholomew, who see me as someone I can only hope someday to be.

It would have been hard to write a book about family without the support of my own. Thanks to my dear parents, Ann and David Bates, who gave me confidence whenever mine lagged and an unconditional love that is inspiring, and to my brother, David Bates, who can always make me laugh. My father-in-law, James Deakin, one of the writers I admire most, has been my relentless and enthusiastic cheerleader. I'm thankful to Doris Deakin, my mother-in-law, too. Your memory left you before I started this book, but I know your spirit is inside it. I've imagined us standing in the waves in North Carolina talking the words through.

Thank you to my sons, Adam and Charlie. It was hard to fly away from you to write about love and family, but so joyous to return. And to my husband, David, thank you for your tremendous generosity of time and support and love. It is no exaggeration to say I could not have done this without you.

I feel so lucky to have Skinner House as the publisher of this book. Thank you, Mary Benard, for your light hand and strong encouragement. Thanks to Ari McCarthy for your tireless work. And thanks to Tom Stites, editor of *UU World*, who was my first contact within the Unitarian Universalist Association. In many ways, you are where this journey started. I'm also indebted to Chris Walton, who first mentioned my name at Skinner House.

Many friends gave me insight and wisdom by reading all or part of the manuscript. Thank you, Gundy, and Chan and Elaine and Deax. And thank you to the Reverend Carlton Elliott Smith, who didn't just read pages but also taught me the connection between intimate journalism and ministry and who gave me the permission I needed to write this book.